£9-50

A Nice Place to Live

A Nice Place to Live

PAMELA SCOTT

Edited by

PHILIP MASON

MICHAEL RUSSELL

First published in Great Britain 1991
by Michael Russell (Publishing) Ltd
Wilby Hall, Wilby, Norwich

Reprinted 1992

Typeset in Palatino by The Spartan Press Ltd
Lymington, Hampshire
Printed and bound in Great Britain
by Biddles Ltd, Guildford and King's Lynn

ISBN 0 85955 180 6

Contents

Author's Foreword

I am a child of two worlds. I was born into a Scottish Border family of which the head, my grandfather, was a Duke, but I came to Kenya when I was four and I have lived in Kenya all my life, drawing my food from Kenya and working with her peoples. I am a hybrid of two cultures, their origins far apart but fundamentally not so different, and the two have become more and more intertwined in my life as I have grown older.

This is the story of how we came to Kenya and how our life developed. I have tried to be as factual as possible and leave the reader to form his own opinion. Many books have been written about Kenya; some are good and some bad. Some are blatant distortions of the truth. That is why I have reluctantly agreed to write this book. Those who criticize the actions of an earlier generation should remember that things looked very different at the time; our forebears had to act in the light of what they then knew and of the opinions people then held.

P.M.D.S.

Editor's Introduction

In *A Nice Place to Live* Pamela Scott tells the tale of a remarkable personal achievement set against an unusual background.

She was only eighteen, with practically no formal education, when her father put her in charge of a farm in Kenya of between three and four thousand acres, on which thirty African families were living. It was quite undeveloped; there were only seventeen cows, hardly any fencing, no piped water. The workers were untrained and illiterate. She had no help in running the farm from her father, who had become immersed in the politics of a rapidly changing country. Forty-five years later, when she sold the farm to the Rift Valley College of Science and Technology, there were five thousand acres, most of it fenced into paddocks with piped water laid on from dams or boreholes. There were 1,700 cattle, the majority Ayrshire–Sahiwal crosses, of which 350 were cows in milk. There was an African manager and an African accountant; the herd records were all kept by Africans; there were over a hundred trained workers living on the farm with their families and dependants, besides old people and former workers; there was a flourishing school and there were young people from this lively community – over a thousand strong – under training for various skills all over the world, many of whom kept in touch with Pamela.

That is a summary of the achievement. What gives it an unusual fascination and excitement is the background against which it is set. First, there is Kenya itself, a country where the combination of strong sun and high altitude produces a peculiar intensity of life, an exaggeration of normal eccentricities, an emotional intensity that comes home to every visitor. Then there is the contrast between life in Kenya and that of Pamela Scott's exalted connections in England and Scotland; behind it all there is her own remarkable character and the glimpses she gives us of the birth of a nation seen through her eyes. One of her grandfathers was the Duke of Buccleuch, the other that Earl of Minto who was Governor-General of Canada and Viceroy of India – and who incidentally rode four times in the Grand National. When in Europe she stayed at Hever Castle with the Astors or at various ducal castles in Scotland; her uncle was the Lord Chamberlain, her grandmother a lady-in-waiting, she went to tea with Queen Mary – but she was always glad to get back to the farm in Kenya. Not that she rebelled either at grandeur or at civilization; she took life in her stride, just as it came, just as she took people for what they were without praise or blame – Masai herdsmen, ducal cousins or the Russian princess who ran her extraordinary finishing school in Paris.

She is singularly reticent about her own fears and desires but gives the impression of having been more frightened of going into the wrong house in Eaton Square during her coming-out season than she ever was of a murderous attack when she slept alone on an isolated farm during the Mau Mau insurrection. It must be significant that she never touched alcohol. 'From early days, when we were sipping and experimenting, she said she didn't like the taste!' That was the memory of a lifelong friend. But in the circles in which she moved it is a taste that most people do acquire and it shows great strength of mind that she did not, though she did not mind others drinking. To me it seems likely that, without knowing it, she had resolved never to lose control of herself. That can only be a guess but it is in keeping with much in her character. Consider the pertinacity she showed in learning book-keeping as well as such arts as diagnosing tick-borne diseases in cattle, delivering calves and castrating young bulls, the elements of building – all the varied skills a farmer needs on an isolated holding in an undeveloped country. She says nothing of her motives but to me gives the impression of a deep inner determination to make a good job of what she had put her hand to. She never puts on an act. She judges by practical standards; to increase the production of food is good and it is good to live in beautiful surroundings, but she does not want to change the customs of the people she has to deal with. In speech I am told she was very outspoken and dismissive of those she thought weak or cowardly. But she understands very clearly the fears of most white settlers at the time of independence as well as the African hunger for land and for freedom from foreign rule. She is quite realistic about the changes coming. But she herself had no hesitation. She was a Kenyan and she was going to stay. She went on farming for another fifteen years after independence and none of the dreadful things happened that had been foretold.

She was a child of two worlds, as she says herself. After independence, she was a member of an agricultural committee who were to be formally introduced to Daniel arap Moi, then Vice-President of Kenya, whom incidentally she knew quite well already. The African chairman introduced her with the words: 'This one looks white, but she is black at heart!' Black at heart! The words might have made a title for her book. Not that for a moment she abandoned her way of living for an African style, but because of her constant interest in things African. As one of her earliest and oldest friends told me: 'When we were quite young and all went to Njoro for our fathers to play polo, Pam would disappear from the mob of children and would be found with the syces, getting them to tell her stories.' She was always interested in the African point of view, in African customs. She took it for granted that people had different customs and standards. Consider the story of how she and Ruth Sladen were attacked on the coast by a man who proved to be mad; very few people would have told that story without saying from the start that he was an African, an Indian or a European. But to Pamela he was just a man.

She became an institution, a Kenya character, the great example of the white settler who had stayed on and made a success of it. Friends asked her to write down her memories – and she agreed because she felt that much had been written about Kenya that was misleading. African friends in particular wanted to know about her family and its history. Soon after she handed over the management of Deloraine in 1979 (she was then sixty-three), she dictated her memories and had them typed. When she says 'now' she means a time early in the eighties. Very few people can dictate without repetition and occasional verbosity; she was advised to have her book edited. It was towards the end of 1989 that I undertook to edit the manuscript and soon afterwards she had a stroke which has prevented any further discussion. She is now in a nursing home in Kenya and is pleased that her book is being published. I am much indebted for help I have had from Elspeth Huxley, Geraldine Macoun, Moyra Smiley, Philip Smiley and Xan Smiley.

I have cut out some repetition and some passages about her parents before they came to Kenya. I have made it a book about Pamela, not about her parents. I have rearranged the opening chapters but I have tried to keep the directness and simplicity of style that is so refreshing. I have resisted a constant temptation to underline what seems to me of special interest but on which Pamela does not comment – such as trusting the two little girls just arrived in Kenya to the care of a Masai male, as yet hardly known, or making a nursery out of the haunted tower in a Scottish castle. And think of Loder, eating by herself year after year! The Edwardian English were as tenacious in transporting overseas the class distinctions they had known at home as Hindus are at exporting the distinctions of caste. Or perhaps the younger sons of English gentlemen who went to

Virginia three hundred years earlier would be a better comparison. They tried to reproduce in America the lives their elder brothers lived, with packs of hounds and colonial mansions – but there were poor whites as well as black slaves and Indians in the forests.

There is a great deal I should have liked to emphasize. Writing of the early explorations of East Africa, she says: 'I often think of what risks the Africans took' – meaning the porters and servants. That is a thought not often to be met in books about the early pioneers. When she was presented at Court – and had to be first, because her uncle was Lord Chamberlain – she was afraid she might 'make a bosh' of the two curtseys she had to make to the King and to the Queen. Fifty years later, she uses just the language she would have used at seventeen. (My daughters at that age would have said 'made a bish'.) She was 'a little put out' when, still only twenty-two or twenty-three, she went to a dance and people asked: 'How are the cows?' 'I thought I must have dung in my hair' she writes. I know just how she felt. When I had been a month in camp among Indian villagers, trying to settle disputes about fields that were life and death to them, I found that for a few days after I came back I could not make small talk about nothing at the club. Some of her dancing partners, she says, again at the same age, were 'not very good dancers' and 'as we trudged round the hot and stuffy room, my mind would sometimes turn . . . to Masai dances under the stars . . .' And think of this recent debutante getting out the after-birth, when a cow retained it – 'always a nasty messy job' she writes. When she is told that a madman on her farm had announced that he was coming up to the house to kill her, her comment is only: 'I thought this rather strange'. I find I like her more and more as I read her memories.

There is no end to the points in her story that I wanted to underline. But I have resisted temptation and introduced only three thoughts of my own, comparisons of one situation with another which Pamela does not make, but to which I am sure she would have agreed. The cattle-stealing exploits of her ancestors on the Scottish borders are recalled when she tells of cattle-stealing in Africa; her own initiation into London society is remembered in connection with the Masai female initiation; her mother's escape, when she was depressed, to the view from the top of the hill above the farm is linked to her own similar retreat when she herself wondered whether all she had done was worth while. But she looks at the landscape with a far more practical eye than her mother! These are my three insertions.

One historical note is needed. It is altogether in keeping with Pamela Scott's character that her account of the Mau Mau emergency should be a good deal less sensational than it might have been in other hands. A visitor to Kenya in that period was likely to be aware of a deep horror below the surface, due, I believe, to the mysterious and unaccountable nature of the movement, the pitiless barbarity of the attacks and extreme obscenity of some of the oaths. There were murders by servants who shortly before had been on friendly and even affectionate terms with their employers. Whole communities were massacred; most of the victims were slashed indiscriminately and often mutilated after death. The worst oaths were clearly intended to put those who had taken them in the power of the movement's leaders and make it impossible for them to go back into any kind of normal society, white or black. It is said that similar oaths have been administered by gangs in the Chicago underworld. The aim of the movement's organizers appears to have been to establish control over the entire Kikuyu people as a first step and only when that was achieved to turn in full strength on Europeans. I feel that to get a full historical picture the reader should, bear this in mind when reading Pamela's chapter on Mau Mau.

It was because of its historical value as a picture of life in Kenya in the early days of the white settlers that my attention was first drawn to this manuscript. I have not said much about this in this introduction, though I think its value considerable. It pictures the life of most settlers – not dissipated socialites but hard-working farmers; it tells of their struggles against ticks and locusts and disease. They found out the hard way what would grow in Kenya and what would not. But, as I worked on her pages, I became far more interested in Pam's character and reactions and the contrasts of her two styles of life.

'I remember her as a strikingly beautiful young woman,' said a man who had known her when he too was young. 'But it was not advisable to take any liberties!' he added ruefully. I have found working on her memories a fascinating task and have tried not to take too many liberties. I believe that many will find pleasure in reading about a life which has indeed been worth living.

PHILIP MASON

PART ONE
Beginnings

1

We Go to Africa

We set sail for Africa on 18 December 1920, when I was four years old and my sister Moy not quite two. My father was in Africa already and the party consisted of my mother, Moy and myself, my mother's Cockney maid Ada Loder, and our nanny Isabel Chalmers. I had been shown photographs of Africa, all in black and white, and had been told that all the people were black so I imagined that we too would turn black in time. This did not worry me, but when I heard that my father was coming to meet us, I suddenly lost my nerve and ran away and hid. I thought he would have turned black already and I was frightened to meet him. But they soon found me and of course he looked just the same as before.

This was when we arrived in Mombasa on 14 January 1921; we were soon on the train for Nairobi, three hundred miles away. In those days there were no restaurant cars so the train used to stop at stations where the passengers could get out and eat. When the grown-ups got out to have dinner, Moy and I were frightened of being left alone in the train; we thought it might go on and leave my parents behind. But Ero, my father's personal servant – 'personal boy' we used to say then – came to be with us and we were soon happy. Ero was a Masai and he went everywhere with my father. Ero was not his real name; all Masai men call each other 'Ero'; it means 'chum' or 'mate'. Ero was a great character and stayed with us for many years. I think he must have left his own people with his mother as a small boy during the 1890 famine, some fifteen years before the British imposed their rule. He came to my father as soon as he arrived in Kenya and we were all very fond of him. Later, when I was naughty, as I often was, and expecting a spanking from my father, I would run away into the forest and Ero was always sent to fetch me back. He used to give me long lectures on what a terrible woman I would grow up to be if I behaved like that and how no would want to marry me and I would not be fit to be the mother of children.

The first morning in the train we woke to find ourselves covered in a film of red dust; it had come up from the ground into the carriage because the line had not been ballasted and it had covered everything. We all looked completely red; so did the luggage, bedding and everything else.

We soon moved out of Nairobi and went to the farm my father had bought, about a hundred and fifty miles away. Here there were two mud huts ready for us, one for my parents, one for Nanny, Moy and me. Loder had a tent. She used to say: 'A hyena came in and licked me fyce one night.' Later, we had two more huts so that my parents could have a bedroom and sitting-room and we could have a day and night nursery. While we still had only one, I remember there was not room for the beds, tables and chairs all at once, so during the day the beds were put outside and the chairs and tables put in; they in turn went out at night to make room for the beds. These huts were round and we lived in them for about two years whilst our new house was being built. I remember the smell of the thatch and the mudded walls. Even now when going into a mud hut it brings back memories of those days. Our huts were better than the usual ones that the Africans lived in, as they had wooden floors, wooden doors and shutters. The walls were plastered with cow dung and ashes. They were very comfortable.

The kitchen was another hut and the cook used to cook on three stones with a pot on top. Baking was done in a hole in the ground filled with hot ashes. The dough was put into a tin and placed in the hot ashes and covered over with more hot ashes. It used to bake very good bread. To wash, we used to have a big tin bath brought into the centre of the hut. *Debes* of hot and cold water were tipped in and we used to sit in this to wash. When we had finished the water would be taken out and tipped onto the flowers and vegetables that we were trying to grow. *Debes* – pronounced 'debbies' – were four-gallon tin cans that were used as containers for most things in those days. Petrol, kerosene and paraffin came in them. They were very useful, because if you cut out the tops when the original contents were finished and fitted a bar of wood as a handle they could be used for carrying water or anything. They came in pairs in a wooden box and these wooden boxes again were most useful for making furniture. If you put one on top of another and then the same about two feet away and covered them with some planks they made a very good dressing table. Or if you wanted to make a chest of drawers, you simply added a few more petrol boxes, fixed them together and nailed a piece of cotton cloth over the front for a curtain and it really looked quite nice. Most of our furniture in those early days on the farm was made out of petrol boxes.

All the water had to be carried up by hand from the nearby spring. To make it fit for drinking we had to boil it and then filter it. We always had a big bonfire outside at night to keep away wild beasts and drifts of smoke would come into the huts. The smell of wood burning and the crackling of the logs were very soothing and I would lie in bed listening to the hyraxes and nightjars. I've always loved the sound of hyraxes; the hyrax is sometimes wrongly called a bush-baby and is about the size of a rabbit or squirrel. But the nightjars used to frighten me. I thought that they were evil spirits that would come and pluck me out of my bed and I used to snuggle right down inside my flea-bag to prevent them. Flea-bags were what we called sleeping bags and we used them on our camp beds. As well as hyraxes and nightjars, we used to hear other animal noises at night, hyenas and occasionally a leopard. Sometimes we heard lions, but I don't remember being frightened by them.

Often African people would come and dance by the fire and I remember the sight of their oiled bodies glistening in the light of the flames with their red braided hair tossing about as they leapt in the air in the dance. They carried spears which they twirled round and round so that they glinted; they had bells on their legs which clashed as they stamped up and down. In those days, when people carried spears though on peaceful errands they used to cover the point with a little leather shield with a black pompom on the top to show that they were coming in peace. I remember an early settler telling me that he could recall the very early days when the Masai used to go on raids. Long before you saw them, you could see the glint of the sun on their spears in the distance. They would jog along, tossing the spears up and down and twisting them so that the sun caught on the blades making flashes like a heliograph.

My parents had bought some local cows for milk and these were milked close to the huts each day. Loder was in charge of the milking and we used to enjoy watching this and seeing the little calves. In those days there was no dipping of cattle and many of the calves would die of tick-borne diseases. The cows would not let down their milk if they did not see their calves; they were Zebu cows, humped Indian cattle who have a very strong maternal instinct. So dead calves had to be skinned and stuffed with straw and these curious-looking objects would be placed in front of the cows' noses and they would lick them and think they were their calves and so let down their milk.

We had chickens to supply us with eggs and Nanny was put in charge of them. She was a girl of about twenty-five from the Border country between Scotland and England; her father was a gardener. Meanwhile, my mother was busy trying to make a garden. She planted a few flowers round the huts and she grew vegetables but she soon found it was more difficult than she had expected. Plants would grow beautifully until some insect or animal would come and eat them and she used to get very disheartened, though she did somehow manage to grow enough for us and occasionally a surplus which she sold in Nakuru. Once one of her marrows was exhibited in a shop window with a label – 'Grown by Lady Francis Scott' – attached to it.

My father soon built stables and bought some horses. He got an old Somali pony for me. He was white and his name was Nyeupe, which means white in Kiswahili. He had been brought down from Somaliland by Berkeley Cole and only had one eye and had nicks in his ears but I thought he was beautiful. I used to go riding on him every day, or rather I used to be led by a syce and followed along behind my parents when they went riding on the farm. Early in my childhood my father employed an old Indian syce, Noor Khan, who was a dear old man. He was a Punjabi Muslim and he had been with my father when he was in India. Why he came to us in Africa, where he must have led such a lonely life, I never understood, but he stayed with us until he died. He taught Moy and me to ride and we always loved being with him. He taught the horses tricks; they had to 'salaam' before they were given any food, which meant that they had to lift one of their forelegs and stamp it on the ground. He taught them all to do this. My father played polo every Sunday. He had made a ground at Njoro. Many of the settlers nearby were ex-army officers; some had been in India and some were really good polo players. Each Sunday, the horses with Noor Khan would walk to Njoro, about fifteen miles away, and we would follow in the old T Model Ford. My father would spend the day playing polo and we would meet most of our neighbours.

Old Nyeupe, my pony, was taught to go in harness and my parents acquired a little governess cart. Nanny used to drive us in this every morning. Of course, there were not many roads in those days, or even tracks fit for wheels, and so we usually went the same way down towards the new railway which was being built to Uasin Gishu. This railway was eventually to reach Kampala and become the main line. I remember seeing thousands of men each carrying a *karai* (a tin basin) on his head full of earth and tipping it out to make the embankments.

After breakfast my mother used to hold a sick parade and all the people on the farm who had anything wrong with them would line up for treatment. Nanny used to help her with this and we would make ourselves useful by tearing up bandages and cutting out pieces of lint and so on. In those days people used to get terrible sores called 'veldt sores'. Wherever you had a scratch or a raw place it would become infected and turn into an ulcer. I can remember we had them all over our arms and legs. The other thing we used to suffer from were jiggers in our toes. Jiggers are little burrowing fleas which live in the dust and get under your toenails; they lay eggs and the place gets very itchy. When we had a jigger, we always had an African to take it out; they were the only people who knew how to remove them properly. They would take a needle or pin, which we used to sterilize with a match, and dig under our toenails and fetch out little sacks of eggs. The art of removing them lay in not breaking the sack containing the eggs or the toe would sometimes go septic. If it was removed successfully and dabbed with iodine, all would be well. I remember the Africans would laugh and say that they could always tell anyone who came from Nyeri because of the way they walked; they waddled along like ducks because their toes were full of jiggers. Apparently there were more jiggers in Nyeri than anywhere else. Nowadays no one seems to suffer from them and I don't know what happened to them. Morning sick parades were quite good training, I suppose, for us children to accustom ourselves to all the nasty sores and wounds we saw and to learn how to help sick people.

Many of the Africans who came to work for us arrived in very poor condition with all sorts of ailments and had to be treated before they were fit to do any work. There was much sickness amongst the babies, usually enteritis or pneumonia and a high death rate. One night a little four-month-old Kavirondo baby died and my mother said how she hated to hear the howling of the hyenas in the night because the Africans threw out their dead to be eaten by them. In fact the Kavirondo used to bury their dead, so my mother need not have worried.

Europeans at that time were terrified of the sun. It was thought that the sun on your bare head would strike you dead and we always had to wear thick topis from eight o'clock in the morning to four o'clock in the afternoon. We were told never to go outside without our topis. We also had to wear spine pads which were quilts lined with red flannel and were pinned to the backs of our dresses to protect our spines. These too were considered essential to prevent sunstroke. We would ask our parents why it was that the Africans could go out without hats and were told that their skulls were so thick that the rays of the sun could not penetrate them. Then we asked them why it was that the Indians did not wear them and were told that the men always wore turbans and the women were veiled and in any case did not go out in the sun much. It was not until the Second World War, when soldiers and sailors went out into the sun without hats, that people realised that one didn't necessarily drop dead from sunstroke and it was only then that white people gave up wearing hats all the time.

My father, though not very mobile because of his wounded leg, used to go pigeon shooting with a shotgun for the pot. I used sometimes to go with him and retrieve the birds that he shot and he taught me to wring their necks when they were not quite dead, and not to mind getting the blood on my hands. He also taught me to crouch down while he shot over my head and not to be afraid of the noise of the gun. I think as children we were rather bloodthirsty; we used to watch when animals that had been killed were cut up, to see if there was a baby inside.

Our nearest neighbours were the Sladens; their children were the same age as we were. There was a boy called Eddie, about two years older than I was, next a girl, Geraldine, just my age, and then Ruth who was Moy's age. So we used to do everything together as we lived very close. Very often we would all go riding together, with a syce. We had been told that when the Africans put out their dead to be eaten, the hyenas would sometimes tear off an arm or leg, carry it away and drop it somewhere. Once there was an African on the Sladens' farm who was killed by a buffalo and so when we were out riding we would keep an eye out for one of his arms or legs. But we never found any. One of my earliest memories was going to the Sladens' kitchen garden where they had a deep hole full of water which they used to water their plants and I leaned over too far and fell in; I had to be fished out by one of their gardeners.

Between the Sladens' huts and ours was a belt of flat-topped thorn trees (*Acacia abyssinica*). There were usually a number of vervet monkeys playing in them. In the midst of this was the Sladens' 'little house' or lavatory. We believed that there was a monstrous wild animal which we called the 'lavatory animal' who lived there, and it was likely to attack us when we had to visit the place. I don't recall how we acquired this idea; I suppose someone had once teased us. We had also been told about the 'Nandi Bear', or 'chemosit' as the Africans called it. This was a mythical animal that was supposed to bite off the tops of peoples' heads and eat their brains. Most African huts are low, and you have to stoop to get out of the door, so the first thing to go out is your head. Therefore, we were told, you should wear a cooking pot on your head, so that the chemosit, if it was lying in wait would only seize the pot in its jaws and not your head. We had an idea that this animal lived under the bridge over the Molo River that we had to cross to leave the farm. Luckily we usually crossed this bridge in the car, and were reasonably safe, but when on horseback we would always sigh with relief if we managed to get over without being attacked.

I remember from our earliest days in Kenya the different kinds of people on the farm – the Masai, who looked after the cattle, the Kikuyu, who had their own little bits of cultivation and the Luo. The Kikuyu used to rub themselves and their clothes, which were skins, with castor oil and this gave them a very acrid smell. We could smell them coming from quite a distance. As children, when walking along the footpaths we couldn't see over the tall grass but we could smell a Kikuyu and we would shout: 'A Kikuyu is coming.' The Kikuyu women wore skirts of skin and we could also hear them coming by the flap, flap, flap of their skirts as they walked. Their arms and legs were bound up in rings of wire and, of course, plenty of beads. Their ears were stretched with various ornaments hanging in them. The Luo went about virtually naked as they didn't wear clothes, just a cloth tied round their waists. They had many marks all over their bodies and I remember being fascinated as a child with all the little bumps and cuts they had on their limbs – cicatrisation it is called. They did their hair in funny patterns, all lines and squares and squiggles all over their heads. They smoked long pipes which were sometimes over two feet long. None of this seemed odd to us. We just accepted that some people were like that and that everyone had their own way of doing things.

2
Who We Were

I should explain who we were and what we were doing in Africa. My father was Francis George Montagu-Douglas-Scott. He was born at Dalkeith Palace near Edinburgh in November 1879 and was the youngest of six sons and two daughters of the 6th Duke of Buccleuch who was also, through an heiress, 8th Duke of Queensberry.

My mother was Eileen Nina Evelyn Sibell Murray-Kynynmound-Elliott. She was born in Ottawa, Canada in December 1884, while her father was on the staff of the Governor-General, Lord Lansdowne. Her father was at that time Lord Melgund, but later succeeded his father and became the 4th Earl of Minto. He in his turn became Governor-General of Canada and later Viceroy of India.

My parents were married in the Guards Chapel in London in February 1915 and I was born in July 1916 and christened Pamela Violet. My sister was born in March 1919; she was Moyra Eileen.

The Scotts – my father's people – and the Elliotts – my mother's – were Scottish Border clans. They had the same background. In the past they had lived in strong stone towers or fortified houses with thatched roofs. Their lives were spent in almost continual fighting, mainly against the English but sometimes clan against clan.

There was continual raiding for cattle. On moonlight nights the men would reach for their spears and ride out across the border and raid and burn the villages, taking back with them what they could – not only cattle, but sometimes women and children as well. It is said that Walter Scott of Harden was one night heard to say, as he rode past a useful-looking haystack: 'By my soul, had ye but four feet ye should not stand there long.' When the store of food was getting low, his wife would serve up a pair of spurs in a dish as a hint that it was time to ride out and fill the larder. Fighting was their life. What they had, they defended by the sword; what they needed, they took by the sword. The women were as tough as the men. On one gravestone is written:

Fair Maiden Lilliard
Lies under this stone,

Little was her stature,
But muckle was her fame.
Upon the English loons
She laid many thumps,
An' when her legs were cutted off
She fought upon her stumps.

With the union of the Scottish and English crowns in 1603, the Borderers were obliged to give up their raids on England but though their lives changed, their characters did not. They were still fighters. Many distinguished themselves as soldiers and sailors.

The Scotts were probably the most powerful of these Border clans. Their chief was Buccleuch. Their stronghold was at Branxholme, near Hawick in Roxburghshire. They lived a wild and unruly life; Captain Walter Scott of Satchells writes:

Lord of Buckcleugh unto the Scots Border
Was High Lord Warden, to keep them in good order.
On that Border was the Armstrongs, able men,
Somewhat unruly and very ill to tame;
I would have no one think that I call them thieves,
For if I did it would be arrant lies,
For all Frontiers and Borders I observe,
Wherever they lie are Freebooters,
And does the enemy much more harms
Than five thousand marshall men in arms . . .

The head of the clan, 'bauld Buccleuch', as he was called, was Warden of the Western Marches. He was knighted by James VI. He was later made a baron and fought in the Netherlands under Maurice Prince of Orange. His son Walter became the 1st Earl of Buccleuch, and his grandson, Francis became the 2nd Earl. This Francis had two daughters, Mary and Anne. The elder, Mary, succeeded to the title as Countess of Buccleuch and at the age of eleven was married to the Earl of Tarras, aged fourteen. But she died two years later, childless, and was succeeded by her sister Anne. Anne was married at the age of twelve to King Charles II's fourteen-year-old son James, Duke of Monmouth, whose mother was Lucy Walters. It remains unproved that Lucy went through any form of marriage with Charles. There is a story in the family that many years later a Duke of Buccleuch did find a marriage contract but burned it in order to avoid trouble.

Anne and the Duke of Monmouth were created Duke and Duchess of Buccleuch and Monmouth and were given various other titles on their marriage. The Duke considered that as a Protestant he was rightful heir to the throne and rebelled against the accession in 1685 of James II, who was a Catholic. The rebellion failed, Monmouth was beheaded and his titles were attaindered, but Anne was allowed to keep hers. She was succeeded by her grandson Francis, the 2nd Duke of Buccleuch, who married Jane Douglas, heiress of the 2nd Duke of Queensberry, who had married the heiress of the Duke of Montagu. In this way the vast possessions of the Dukes of Montagu and Queensberry came to the Scott family, who took the name Montagu-Douglas-Scott. William, the 6th Duke, was my grandfather.

My grandmother was Louisa Jane Hamilton (called 'Tiny' by her family), daughter of the 1st Duke of Abercorn. She was one of thirteen children, and her mother Louisa Russell, a daughter of the Duke of Bedford, was reputed to have over one hundred and twenty descendants when she died. Aged four, Louisa Russell had danced on a table at Brighton before King George IV. Her mother was Georgiana, daughter of the 4th Duke of Gordon and Jennie Maxwell. As a child Jennie Maxwell and her sisters are said to have ridden pigs down the wynds in Edinburgh. After her marriage to the Duke of Gordon, she created a sensation by going to a Court ball in London dressed in tartan, which was then not only proscribed as a dress for political reasons but was also considered fit only for barelegged Highland savages. However, as she was a beautiful young duchess, others followed her example and the tartan became all the rage. Jennie and her daughters helped to raise the Gordon Highlanders in 1794 by travelling round Scotland in their tartan dresses offering recruits sovereigns from their lips.

My father was the youngest of eight children. His parents lived in various big houses – Dalkeith, Bowhill near Selkirk, Drumlanrig Castle and Langholm Lodge in Dumfriesshire, Boughton House in Northamptonshire and Montagu House in Whitehall, London. All these houses were ready for occupation at all times. The family and their personal servants would move from one to the other; to Dalkeith and Bowhill in the winter, Langholm and Drumlanrig in the autumn, and Boughton and Montagu House in the summer. Wherever they were, the household was enormous; apart from the family, there were always numerous friends and relatives staying; my father had eighty-four first cousins. There was a large household staff, because in those days there was no running water, electric light or central heating, so besides the usual butlers, footmen, maids and cooks there were lamplighters, water-carriers and firemakers as well. There would probably be sixty or seventy people living in the house at one time. Servants had long hours, hard work and small pay but seem to have led a happy and sometimes eventful life in a large household of that kind. 'Service' was much sought after by people on the estate.

My father was brought up by his beloved nurse 'Ordie' in the nursery and saw little of his parents. When he did see them, it was an ordeal; he had to be dressed in a velvet suit with a lace collar and until he was six had long golden hair which he disliked and eventually managed to have cut off by subterfuge. He would be taken to the drawing-room and had to be on his best behaviour. He was not on intimate terms with his mother until he was much older. When he asked her to play with him, she used to say: 'Not now, darling, I am busy writing a letter to the Queen.'

She was Mistress of the Robes to Queen Victoria and must have been very busy with such a large family and household to look after as well. When he was about seven he used to go out hunting with a groom on a pad without stirrups – which was supposed to improve his grip – and he used to tell how tired he got. As the youngest of six brothers, when he went out shooting with them in the hills, he had to carry the hares and birds they had shot. He said they seemed very heavy after a few miles in the heather.

They were a happy family. Their great loves were shooting, hunting and cricket. My father played cricket for Eton as did some of his brothers. They used to have a family team of whatever brothers were available, made up with footmen and grooms. His father had his own pack of fox-hounds and the shooting was then the best in Scotland. In 1911 they got what was then the record bag of grouse in Scotland in one day, 2,523. They lived among the most beautiful art treasures, which they never appreciated. They used the most rare and valuable objects as goalposts for football in the passages. When one Duke was shown round the Louvre by its Director, the latter is supposed to have said, 'Monsieur le Duc, I apologise for our furniture.'

It was a happy life for a boy. My father spent much time with keepers and grooms and the people of the estate, and all his life he enjoyed the company of people from all walks of life. After Eton he went to Oxford, but when the Boer War broke out he left and joined the Grenadiers, much to his father's annoyance; he said he had sons in the Army and Navy and wanted one to go into the Church. My father described his time in South Africa as 'chasing on foot after Boers on horseback'. But he enjoyed it, he said, and it was then that he fell in love with Africa.

After the South African War he spent a year or two with his regiment in London until he was asked by Lord Minto to go on his staff in India as an aide-de-camp. He accepted and spent the next five years there. This greatly influenced his life. My father always admired Lord Minto – later his father-in-law – and he was able to see fine administrators at work and learn something of how a country was ruled. He then had another spell of soldiering, interrupted by some months in Canada as aide-de-camp to the Duke of Connaught, until the outbreak of the 1914 war.

The Elliots had a similar background to the Scotts. Their home was at Minto in Roxburghshire. The first Sir Gilbert Elliot of Minto was made a baronet in 1700. After a stormy youth he became a Lord of Session, as was his son, the second Sir Gilbert. His daughter Jean is famous for writing the song 'The Flowers of the Forest' for a bet, but she never wrote anything else. The third Sir Gilbert's son became the 1st Earl of Minto. He was Governor-General of India, and had distinguished himself in many other positions. He died on his way back from India to Minto. Stories are told that his ghost can be seen in the Minto woods. The 2nd Lord Minto was Ambassador to Berlin, Lord of the Admiralty and Lord Privy Seal, and the 3rd Lord Minto also followed a political career. His son Gilbert, known as 'Rolly' to his friends from the way he walked, was my mother's father, and became the 4th Earl of Minto and the second Minto to be Governor-General of India.

He was born in 1845 and spent his early years at Minto. He enjoyed rough country pursuits, hunting or shooting all day in all weathers or standing in the river up to his waist fishing in freezing water. At the same time his mind was early broadened by listening to good talk; there were frequent discussions on books and politics at Minto. At Eton however he was more distinguished for rowing and running than for academic learning. After Eton he went to Cambridge, where he did much hunting and race-riding. His joy in life was horses. After Cambridge he was commissioned in the Scots Guards, but found soldiering not to his taste; his heart was on the racecourse. So he sent in his papers and went to Limber to ride under the name of 'Mr Rolly' for Mr Cat Richardson. There he dedicated his life to riding. He never bet, as he thought it spoilt the sport; nor did he smoke or drink. He rode at most of the meetings in different parts of England, four times in the Grand National and nine times altogether over the Liverpool course. Many years later when making a speech to the Turf Club in Calcutta, he said: 'I do not regret my racing days – very far from it; I learned a great deal from them which has been useful to me in later life. I mixed with all classes of men. I believe I got much insight into the human character. In the ups and downs of racing I learned to keep my head, to sit still and be a good judge of pace.'

In 1876 he had a very bad fall in the Grand National when he broke his neck, and he was not able to ride regularly in races after that. He did not care for London society life. 'Everyone on their p's and q's,' he wrote, 'especially the politicals, who are oppressed with their own importance, but there is not one of them fit to take a horse to a second class metropolitan meeting and look after him. He would do something silly if he mingled on an equality with his fellow men.' He was still interested in soldiering and was given command of the newly formed Border Mounted Volunteer Corps recruited from Border lairds and farmers. But he was always on the lookout for other interests and activities. He went to India with Lord Roberts, he went to Turkey, South Africa and Egypt. He gained insight into the world and the men in it. He was also a good mountaineer. In 1883 he married Mary Grey, daughter of General the Honourable Charles Grey, and not long afterwards they went to Canada in Lord Lansdowne's staff. Here he saw the business of government. One of his first tasks was to recruit three hundred *'voyageurs'* to act as steersmen for the Nile boats that were to go to the relief of General Gordon in Khartoum. They were half-caste Indians who were experts in paddling birchbark canoes.

In 1898 he was appointed Governor-General of Canada, and at the end of the year he went there with his family. Canada was then rising in importance. There was development and expansion and zest. The life was just to the Minto family's taste. The scenery – the mountains, rivers and forests – all delighted them. Minto's great physical fitness and capabilities were admired by the Canadians and he was a good mixer.

But the political world was unfamiliar. He had to contend with party politics and the problem of defence, which was complicated by the Boer War; there was the French-Canadian question, the relationship of Canada with Britain and with the USA (especially over Alaska), and the problem of administration of the American Indians, for whom he had particular sympathy. He had seen on his travels that the best results in administering such people came from a wise tolerance, when a harsh hand would have led to strife. When the Indians complained to him that the missionaries were stopping them dancing, he said he could not see why, as their dances were much tamer than the Scottish reels.

Minto was six years in Canada; his term of office was extended by a year. He returned with his family to Scotland in 1904. To be back home after his busy life was a joy, but it was not to last long. In August 1905 he heard he had been nominated Viceroy of India in succession to Lord Curzon. 'The greatest appointment I have ever hoped for,' he wrote in his journal, 'but it is a very high trial.' Lord Curzon was said to be much annoyed at being succeeded by a 'gentleman who can only jump hedges'.

Minto said: 'I don't know much about India but I do know that a horse sometimes needs a rest in his gallops.' He must have thought Lord Curzon had been apt to overtrain.

The office of viceroy was in those days perhaps the most demanding of any in the Empire. India was a huge country of many diverse peoples and all important decisions had to be taken personally by the viceroy. The work was immense, the pomp and ceremony fantastic. There were over six hundred servants in the Government House alone. Minto immediately established good relations with Gokhale, the leader of the Congress Party – later the party of Nehru and Gandhi. His key word was 'sympathy'.

As to Congress [he wrote] we must recognize and be friends with the best of them. I wonder if it would ever be possible to start a small club with both British and Indian members. If we could only get more in touch with the people with whom we live. But with all one's desire for sympathy we must not lose sight of the hard facts. We are here in a small British garrison surrounded by millions composed of factions of an inflammability unknown to the Western World, unsuited to Western government, and we must be physically strong or go to the wall.

Though Minto was of a liberal cast of mind, it has been written that he was the last viceroy to take it for granted that Britain would uphold her rule if necessary by force. After the First World War it was generally recognized that the ultimate goal was independence. It soon became obvious to Minto that reforms to give Indians some voice in government were needed. The chief reform was the enlargement of the Legislative and Executive Councils so that some Indian members could be appointed to them. There was fierce opposition to this, but Minto got his way and what became known as the Morley-Minto Reforms were enacted.

The physical strain of five tumultuous years in India was huge but Minto found time to shoot and ride. He was probably the only viceroy to ride in the show-jumping competitions, once completing the course after a fall. He loved riding at the head of a large military parade on a beautiful Arab stallion, galloping rather faster than some of the generals enjoyed. Not long before his term of office ended Lord Minto said:

We passed through five eventful years . . . As my knowledge of the state of public affairs has increased, I have become more and more aware of a sullen and widespread dissatisfaction and discontent. There was much political unrest quite apart from revolutionary sedition. What were the causes? They were due, to the best of my belief, to the ripening of the educational seed which British rule has systematically sown, and so to me it seems that our recognition of these results has not come a moment too soon, and that it has saved India from many troubles.

The man in the street has cried out for 'strong measures'; I have heard a good deal of 'strong measures' in my time, and I can only say that in my experience the strongest man is he who is not afraid of being called weak.

The strain was indeed great and Minto returned to Scotland in 1910 a tired man. In 1913 he had a bad fall out hunting and died a few months later.

My maternal grandmother, Mary Grey, also came from a Border family, but from the English side. Her family home was at Howick, near Alnwick in Northumberland. The 1st Earl Grey had been a soldier and had gained fame in the war of the American Revolution, as well as in battles against the French.

The 2nd Earl was the Whig Prime Minister of the 1832 Reform Bill. He had fifteen legitimate children and one by Georgiana, Duchess of Devonshire, who was brought up with the others. She is said to have been sent to live with her father by her mother on his wedding day. His second son Charles was the father of Mary, my grandmother. Charles was a general, and became private secretary to the Prince Consort and later to Queen Victoria. He married Caroline, daughter of Sir Thomas Farquhar, Bt. The Farquhars are supposed to be descended from John Rolfe and the Red Indian girl Pocahontas, whom he married in Virginia in 1614. Mary Grey was born in 1859 and brought up at Windsor Castle and St James's Palace, where her parents had rooms. She used to tell how, when the Prince Consort died, her nurse hung a picture of him, framed in black, around her neck. She was taken to tea with one of the princesses in the nursery; the Queen came in, saw the picture and burst into tears. Poor little Mary was hurried away in disgrace.

Mary had a series of governesses of various nationalities. She did no lessons after she was thirteen but became a most knowledgeable and cultured woman and after her marriage to Minto led a very full life. She had a good brain, a great sense of humour and much charm. In India she started the Minto Nursing Association which was a great boon to many. Later she became a lady-in-waiting to Queen Mary. She died in 1940.

My mother spent her early years mainly at her beloved Minto with short visits to Howick. She would go to London in the summer. From her governesses, mostly French and German, she gained a good knowledge of those languages. Hers was a happy family. She was the eldest, then came Ruby who later married the 2nd Earl of Cromer, and Vi, who first married Charlie Mercer-Nairne, the Marquess of Lansdowne's son and after he was killed in the First World War, John Astor, the 1st Viscount Astor's son, who was later created Lord Astor of Hever. Next were the two boys, Larry, who became the 5th Earl of Minto and Esmond who was killed in the First World War. Her journals tell of walks and rides in the beautiful country around Minto, visits to the people in Minto village (usually with little presents of food and clothing), and sitting and reading to those who were ill on the estate. One entry reads:

Frau and I went see the poor consumptive garden boy. I had a shock to see how extremely thin he was, he looks like a skeleton. I couldn't sleep the whole night 'cause I couldn't get him out of my head.

When she was thirteen her father became Governor-General of Canada where she had been born and where she now spent six gloriously happy years. It was then that she began to show talent for acting, and the family and staff did many amateur theatricals. She also became an excellent skater. The family travelled all over Canada; it was a wonderful life for a young girl. When she was twenty the family moved to India. To be viceroy was an onerous task, but to be a viceroy's daughter was enthralling. She had everything a girl could wish for. The three sisters were beautiful and talented, all with high spirits. They became known as the 'three destroying angels'. They had all inherited their father's love of horses and had a stable full of the best in India. There was a large staff at their beck and call, and many rumours of romance with the aides-de-camp, among whom was my father. There were amateur theatricals, dances and balls; shooting too, and my mother once shot a tiger. They travelled in great state all over India. To be continually surrounded by people of talent, the eminent men and women of the day, was enriching and they never ceased to take a deep interest in all that went on in the world.

After returning to England in 1910, my mother travelled a good deal and also did a course at RADA, the Royal Academy of Dramatic Art, taking the name of Mary Montagu. In February 1915 she married my father and lived in London while he was soldiering there, until they decided to settle in Kenya.

It had not taken long for my family to give up their habits of cattle-lifting and border warfare and to become respectable pillars of the state.

3
Why Kenya?

But why Kenya? My father seems to have been attracted by all he heard. It was a very young country – and all kinds of people went there in those early days. Some were remittance men, that is, their families were prepared to pay them allowances so long as they did not come home. One man was sent a telegram by his exasperated elder brother saying: 'Will pay you £10,000 if you will be castrated.' The answer came back 'Will take £5,000 for one!' Others were addicted to the bottle, and it was said that once a snake had bitten a Kenya settler but had died from alcoholic poisoning. Others were fugitives from justice and one man was said to be wanted for murder in seven countries. The immoral goings-on in the Happy Valley of a few notorious people will always be remembered. But the majority were ordinary, hard-working, law-abiding people who only wanted to make a new home for themselves and their families. They saw what appeared to be huge areas of fertile land, almost completely empty, producing nothing, and young Africans sitting idling the day away while their women tilled a few patches of land for their daily food. It was an invitation for someone ready to work.

It was all very new. Only in the middle of the nineteenth century had the first Europeans reached the interior of East Africa. These were not settlers. The first were German missionaries who went far enough to be able to see that Mount Kenya and Kilimanjaro were snow-covered (though nobody believed them). After the missionaries came the explorers, then the hunters and traders. They would go to Zanzibar, with the equipment that they had brought from Europe by ship, and there set about engaging people to go on safari with them. ('Safari' in Kiswahili means a journey, however long or short, and for any purpose.) The first and most important requirement was a good headman; almost everything would depend on him. They had to have enough porters to carry their personal belongings as well as trade goods which they needed to barter for food and also for permission to pass through certain territories. Then they had to have reliable askaris, or guards. Altogether, they might need two or three hundred people, many of whom had previously travelled with the Arabs into the interior on slaving or trading safaris.

The Europeans who organized these expeditions had often never been in Africa before. They could not speak the languages and did not know the ways of the people. All the bad hats of Zanzibar would try to get taken on, but a good headman was usually able to sift the good from the bad. Often I think of what risks the Africans took when they joined a safari in charge of a European about whom they knew nothing. They would have to be prepared to go to unknown places with him, sometimes for several years and though they were paid a part of their wages before they left, the bulk would be paid only on return. They would have to rely on him to shoot for meat and feed them, to look after them in sickness and administer justice whilst in the bush. Punishment was usually by flogging; there was no other way you could punish people far from courts or jails. There were bound to be a few thieves or malingerers amongst such a large party and it was important that no one should loot crops or stock or rape women in places through which they passed. If they made enemies of the local people, they were far from any help.

The goods that had to be carried must then be divided into sixty-pound loads, which was the regulation weight for one man to carry – and they must be fairly distributed. There were no accurate maps, and the only information that could be had was verbal and often inaccurate. Furthermore, they would sometimes reach a place where they had been told there was always food, only to find that the people were starving. There had been a raid by enemies, locusts had eaten everything, or the rain had failed. It was then that they had to rely on their guns to shoot enough meat to feed everyone.

The usual routine on safari was to break camp at dawn and move about ten or twelve miles; it would then be ten or eleven in the morning, camp would be put up again and the rest of the day was spent writing up notes, hunting or doing the daily chores that need to be done in a camp. How far you went in a day depended largely on where there was water, and sometimes in places like the Taru Desert the early travellers had to go forty miles without water. If it was possible they would take donkeys to carry water, and sheep, goats and cattle for food. But where there were tsetse flies this was impossible. The first few days were the most difficult as there were bound to be teething troubles with the loads and organization and desertions were frequent. Once they had gone some distance from their base it was virtually impossible for anyone to desert and survive. There was much illness, especially among the Europeans, who had little resistance to the local diseases and little knowledge about how they were transmitted. They used to get what they called 'fever and dysentery', not distinguishing between malaria, bilharzia, tick typhus and other illnesses. They had very little in the way of medicine, and what they had was not very effective. Often they became so weak that they had to be carried and some died. Injury by wild animals was another hazard, especially whilst hunting.

This is not the place to describe the 'Scramble for Africa' amongst the European nations at the end of the nineteenth century. When it was over, the British found themselves administering a Protectorate in Uganda, as well as the land between Uganda and the coast, a distance of some eight hundred miles. It was decided to build a railway, which became known as the 'Lunatic Line', because there was next to nothing to carry on it. The Africans at that time produced only enough for their own needs, so after a good many arguments in the British Parliament, it was decided to give out some of the land near the line of rail to Europeans to farm. The land seemed to be empty, except for wild animals, and looked fertile and healthy. There had been a plague of smallpox and rinderpest in the 1890s and this had made the country appear more empty than normal. But nothing much happened at first.

Then in 1897 Lord Delamere went on a shooting trip in Somalia and he decided to explore to the south west. He came eventually to the Laikipia Plateau, where he fell in love with the Kenya Highlands and determined to devote his life to developing them into a 'white man's country'. He felt sure all this empty but fertile land could be made productive and that only Europeans could do it. Lord Delamere was an impulsive man who did not easily put up with opposition; he was wealthy and when he wanted to do something he did it in a big way. He started by acquiring a large tract of land from the Government and proceeded to sell up his English property in order to develop this piece of raw Africa. He brought out pedigree sheep and cattle and started planting wheat and other crops. Of course he had many failures – not knowing anything about the various diseases and pests that he had to contend with or the vagaries of the weather. But he never lost faith in the country. He was instrumental in starting the creameries, 'unga' – the flour-milling business; the word means flour – the native industrial training centres to train local artisans, and many other projects from which Kenyans are still benefiting today. Often he financed these projects with his own money and when he died of a heart attack in 1931, far from having made a fortune he owed his creditors huge sums of money. He was the leader of the European settlers almost until he died.

Kenya was originally known as British East Africa or BEA and only later given the name Kenya. It lies astride the Equator; to the north are the arid plains of the proud Somali people, and the mountainous ancient kingdom of Ethiopia; to the west is the huge Lake Victoria Nyanza from which flow the waters of the Nile at the start of their long journey through swamps and deserts to the Mediterranean. To the south are the steppes of the Masai, stretching across the border into Tanzania, with a kink around the northern side of Mount Kilimanjaro. During the Scramble for Africa, the Kaiser wanted to have the biggest mountain in Africa in his territories and it is said that his grandmother, Queen Victoria, gave it to him for his birthday. To the east is the Indian Ocean. From north to south, right down the centre of the country, is a huge crack, the great Rift Valley, which has its beginnings as far away as Israel and stretches far away to the south.

Kenya took its name from the second highest mountain in Africa. There are many stories about this name but the one I like best is this. When Joseph Thomson, an early explorer, was on his travels in 1885, he woke one morning and saw the sun rise behind this snow-covered mountain. He asked one of the Masai with him: 'What is that?' The Masai, thinking he was asking about the sunrise, replied 'Ndadegenya', which is Masai for dawn. Thomson thought he said 'Tadwa Kenia' which means 'Look at Kenia', and he therefore thought the mountain was called Kenia, which it never was.

The local vernaculars have names for the mountain, none of which resembles Kenia. It was first spelt Kenia, the first syllable pronounced to rhyme with 'hen', but later it became known as Kenya and the 'e' made to rhyme with 'bean'. That is how Europeans pronounced it, although Africans usually pronounce it in the former way. Some people think that Jomo Kenyatta took his name from the country, but this is not so. He was nicknamed 'Kenyatta' because he always wore a beaded belt when speaking at meetings and this is called a *kinyata* in Kikuyu.

Kenya is a land with an amazing number of different ecological zones in a relatively small area. The altitude varies from sea level to over 17,000 feet at the top of Mount Kenya and the rainfall from only a few inches a year to over seventy inches in some parts of the Highlands. At the coast grow coconuts and other palms and tropical fruits like mangoes. In the wet country are tea gardens, and in between are open savannahs where wheat, maize, cattle and sheep flourish. In the mountains daffodils and other spring flowers will bloom. But the largest area – about 80 per cent of the country – is semi-desert, occupied only by nomads, with their camels, goats and a few of the hardiest of cattle and sheep.

The Colonial Government divided the country into different areas for different groups. There were the native reserves in which only people of a certain tribe could own land and live; this was partly for their own protection and partly to put the land to good use. As far as possible each tribe was given the area it already occupied. In a sense the Masai were masters of most of the country, because they raided everywhere and were generally feared. But they were nomads and could certainly not be said to occupy everywhere they raided. A treaty was made with them and after a few false starts, it was eventually agreed which land should be theirs and which given out for settlement. What was not native reserve was Crown land and included forest reserve. Only people of European descent could own land in certain areas designated for settlement, which became known as the 'White Highlands'. It is wrong to say that the Europeans took all the best land. The nature of the terrain varied greatly: some was untouched forest, with very fertile soil; some was open land in good rainfall areas, some was dry prairie suitable only for ranching, and some was semi-desert scrub, with very little rainfall. Some settlers were attracted to one kind of land, and some to another, but in the early days little was known by the Europeans about what would grow where and many mistakes were made.

Before the Europeans came, the native people had always been on the move, sometimes to escape enemies or after some disease or pestilence, but even without disasters they would move onto fresh ground after a few years when the fertility of the soil was exhausted or the grazing was insufficient. There was a very high death rate in both people and stock and there were terrible famines caused by droughts, locusts, plague, smallpox and rinderpest. Sometimes people lost everything and had to take refuge in the forest to live by hunting wild animals and gathering wild fruits and vegetables. There were continual raids between the different groups of people, and in some places this was made worse by the slave trade, organized by Arabs from the coast.

The people of the interior had no written history, not surprising among people always on the move. They had no caste of priests or scribes. They felt no need of wheeled transport; there were no roads other than cattle tracks and footpaths. All they had could be carried by headload or by donkey.

When the British divided the land, it meant that people could no longer move around as in the past. This changed their whole way of life. The first safari parties had been given a friendly reception; it is an African custom to welcome strangers and give them food and somewhere to sleep. They would only stay a short time and move on. Now it became clear that there was a new kind of *Wazungu* as Europeans were called, who were planning to stay and who soon started giving orders, telling people what they must do and that they must move here or there. The people resented this and sometimes refused to comply but they soon found that they were liable to be shot or taken prisoner. I once heard Kenyatta in a speech describe what happened in simple terms. He said that when a visitor comes to your house, you feed him and give him somewhere to sleep – but what do you do when after a few days he tells you that the house is his and you can sleep on the floor, while he has the bed?

As a child, I remember being told by old Africans that when the Europeans first came the people thought they looked horrible. They appeared to have been skinned alive; all the black skin had been removed and only the raw flesh left. Or perhaps their pallid colour was because they had milk in their veins, not blood? They had prominent grey-looking eyes, like a sheep, and lank hair, more or less colourless, like the switch of a cow's tail; their noses stuck out like that on a decomposed corpse and their faces were speckled like a snake. They must be ashamed of their bodies because they hid them as much as possible under clothes.

Soon some of the more cunning Africans realized that it would be useful to have these powerful people on their side when it came to fighting their enemies and they started to cooperate with them. On the whole there was very little resistance. The Nandi did skirmish with the British for a few years but after their leader was shot, they too gave in. There were skirmishes with the Kikuyu from time to time, but by the time the settlers started coming in appreciable numbers they met with virtually no opposition. Of course many of the new settlers did not intend to farm; there were businessmen and professional people and missionaries, as well as skilled craftsmen, although the latter were usually Asians. They had no direct influence on the alienation of land. The Asians had been trading on the coast and further inland for many years before there was any European settlement and there was a further influx of them when coolies, on contracts for a certain length of time, were brought in to build the railway. Shopkeepers came to feed the coolies and stayed on.

I do not suppose that many of the settlers gave much thought to what effect their settling on the land would have on the local people. All they wanted to do was to get their farms going and develop their land. To do this they needed labour and they wanted young African men to come and work for them. If anyone had asked one of them how he thought the coming of settlers would effect the Africans, he would have thought it a stupid question. He would have said something like this: 'Well, it can only do good. There will be the Pax Britannica and it will put an end to all the small inter-tribal wars that have been going on; it will be safe for a man or even a woman to walk alone from one end of the country to the other. There will be hospitals when they get sick and schools where they will learn European skills, and contact with Europeans must benefit them as they will learn the ways of civilization.' At that time, remember, British people had been taught that the British way of life was the best in the world and most of them were unquestioning Christians. They thought that to bring Christianity to the people would be doing them a great service. The missionaries hoped to 'save the souls' of the people and to teach them how to live a new life.

By 1914 there were already European settlers who had started to develop their farms. Kenya was being administered by the British, while further south in Tanganyika the Germans were doing much the same. When the First World War broke out, the able-bodied European men rushed to join up and many farms were either altogether abandoned or left in the care of the farmers' wives or African headmen. There was fighting early in the war between the British and Germans all along the border, which does not lie very far to the south of the railway; after the Armistice German East Africa was handed over to the British as a Mandate and known as Tanganyika until it became Tanzania after its union with Zanzibar in 1964.

Quite a number of British settlers who were ex-Army officers went from Kenya to Britain to fight and met my father there. He had gone to France in the Grenadier Guards at the start of the First World War; he was wounded at the Battle of Mons and awarded a DSO. As he was unable to return to France to fight, he was given command of the Depot Battalion at Chelsea Barracks in London. This meant that all officers joining the regiment would come under his command until they were posted. Many distinguished people were amongst them, and later he liked to say that Field-Marshals Lord Alexander and Lord Gort as well as Harold Macmillan had been his subalterns. Several of these young officers came from Kenya. My father was impressed with their love for the country and their longing to get back there. As I have said, he already had a liking for Africa.

He had been shot through the sciatic nerve and had no future in the Army. He had been left with very little money after his father had died, as was customary for younger sons in Britain, and he decided that he would not be able to live in England in the way he had before the war. He therefore applied for a soldier settler farm in British East Africa, which he was lucky enough to get. He thought that there he would be able to do most of the things he liked doing and might with luck make some money as well. These farms were more or less drawn at random on a map. You had to put your name in a hat and see what you pulled out; it was said that one farm was the summit of Mount Kenya! You then had to pay so much down and guarantee to do so much development in a certain time. Many years later, when he was asked why he had come to live in Kenya, and what he had thought he would do there, he replied that he had no idea, but that it seemed a nice place to live.

4
Buying the Farm

My parents made up their minds to go to East Africa and have a look round with a view to settling. It was easier, just after the war, to get a passage to Bombay than to Mombasa, so they went first to India and spent six weeks visiting their old haunts. They sailed on my father's fortieth birthday, 1 November 1919, accompanied by my mother's maid, Miss Ada Loder. She had been my Aunt Violet Astor's parlourmaid in London during the war. She was a real Cockney, though she used to say her uncle had been Mayor of Birmingham. She had gone into service as soon as she had left school, always 'in the best 'ouses', she would tell you. It was the custom to call lady's maids by their surnames without a prefix, so she was always known simply as 'Loder'.

After staying with various friends in India, both British and Indian, my parents left Bombay for Mombasa. They had been pleased to find that Lord Minto was remembered with affection and my father was confirmed in Lord Minto's opinion about the need for sympathy and understanding. He was very conscious of the importance of incidents, however slight they might appear, which might make an Indian feel slighted or humiliated. India was just about to embark on the second stage of the reforms, begun ten years before by Morley and Lord Minto. My father foresaw many difficulties and though he did not doubt reforms were necessary, he did wonder whether Montagu and Chelmsford were quite big enough for the job.

The voyage to Mombasa was uneventful and they were able to continue with their lessons in Kiswahili from a passenger who had lived in East Africa for some years and who had started to teach them on the way out to India. They arrived in Mombasa on 13 January and were struck by the beauty of the harbour – the blue water, with 'inky black natives' paddling dug-out canoes, as well as a number of small sailing boats, and, beyond, flowering trees and shrubs with little white houses with red roofs amongst them. On the other hand they were surprised at how undeveloped the port was: no wharves or docks and the roads on the island just tracks deep in the sand. They spent two nights in the Manor Hotel which they found quite comfortable, though my mother complained about the 'huge flying beetles' that got into her mosquito net. She said my father laughed at her as she was afraid to squash them between her finger and thumb, but she writes: 'I have not yet risen to those heights of courage!'

They then took the train to Nairobi and woke early in the morning to see the game they had been told would be near the line. They were disappointed not to see a lion, though they did see a number of other animals which they were not knowledgeable enough to identify. They were met in Nairobi by Freddie Ward whose wife Vi was a daughter of a former Governor, Sir Henry Belfield. My father had known him in the Army and he put them up in his guest cottage at Muthaiga, just outside Nairobi. Then they set about buying a Model T Ford and getting camping equipment together. They visited various farms, mostly coffee, but thought life as a coffee farmer would be dull. They were, however, much impressed by how well everything grew and how mature plants looked even when only a few years old.

My father went to stay with Mervyn Ridley at his farm, Santamor, at Makuyu. Mervyn was an ex-Grenadier; his sister was Lady Cranworth whose husband had a number of interests in the Colony and had come out before the war to work on a farm. He had been mauled by a lion and had a stiff arm, so the Africans called him 'Mwanguru' meaning a withered arm in Kikuyu. He had made a polo ground and had a small pack of hounds and my father was able to play polo and hunt. He wrote of this place:

> . . . the most glorious view I have ever seen. One can see for miles in every direction, with snow capped Mt Kenia in front, towering over one at about fifty miles distant but looking much closer; then Mt Kinankop on the left and Donyo Sabuk on the right and vast undulating stretches of land on each side . . . It was very lovely; coffee and sisal is growing all around, the latter looks like a cross between a pineapple and a cactus

My father said he had never enjoyed himself so much. Later Mervyn Ridley was to become one of his greatest friends in Kenya.

Meanwhile my mother had been taken to tea with some people called Elkington near Nairobi. She found it

> . . . a delightful place with a number of fit-looking horses and fierce dogs, and also they had a huge male lion in a very feeble-looking cage, an enormously powerful-looking animal which I should very much dislike to meet on foot! Mrs Elkington had had him since a baby; given her by Lord Kingston. She went up to him and

patted his huge paws, but when Mr Elkington went near him he got up and roared at him in the most savage way. I think they are the most unsuitable animals to have as pets.

Both my parents were startled by the way people dressed. My mother wrote: 'None of the men wear a coat, just a shirt all open at the neck and khaki trousers, with a knife and a bunch of keys in a belt.' My father describes one lady who wore shorts and a shirt and had bobbed hair and a double terai: 'she looked like a lady of the chorus at the Alhambra who ought to come in with a hayrake in her hand and throw wisps of hay about.' Another in immaculate boots and breeches and a shirt looked 'the devil of a hard rider', but told him she never rode. 'A very horsey woman on foot,' he remarks. He heard that it was Lady Idina Gordon who started these fashions and he thought she had 'done a lot of harm in the country and behaved like a barmaid'. (She eventually married five times – her third husband was the Earl of Erroll sadly remembered for having been murdered, a decade after he and Idina had divorced – and at the end of her life was living with a man who was known as 'James VI'. She and her friends came to be known as the 'Happy Valley Crowd' and were notorious in Kenya and elsewhere.) My father notes that the country is still very primitive, and that the white people are 'rather casual and slipshod', as well as 'unnecessarily uncomfortable'. The natives, he thought, were 'very unreliable and need personal supervision all the time'. He wondered if it would not be a good plan to bring over some good Indian servants. He went on to say:

> There is no doubt that this country will go ahead as soon as it can get enough capital, but at present it is all held up because of the bad exchange . . . I hope that they will put us on a sterling basis and have done with it. It requires a lot of money for roads, railways and the development of the harbour at Mombasa. Once that is done the country is so naturally rich as an agricultural land that it must go ahead.

At first the currency in British East Africa had been the rupee and the rate of exchange with London was the same as for the Indian rupee. Soon after the war the rupee was devalued and many people in East Africa were hard hit, as most of them had borrowed money and they woke up one day to find that they had to repay twice as much as they had bargained for.

My parents took the train to Nakuru on 23 January and were enthralled by the wonderful views and the beautiful country that they travelled through, especially the Rift Valley and the mountains in the distance. After spending the night at Nakuru they motored on to Kishobo near

Njoro where they camped near the house of Sandy Wright, who was Lord Delamere's agent. They had taken Loder with them and they found her invaluable in the camp coping with the washing and cooking. They made several expeditions to different farms and went as far as Ravine, Bahati and Solai and had some meals with some of the settlers. They thought some of their houses and food excellent but could not get over how little trouble most of them took to make themselves comfortable; the filth at some of the places was terrible. My mother says that only hunger and thirst forced her to drink out of the dirty glasses and eat off the cracked plates! They also went to a dance at somebody's house and my mother found it very difficult to dress for a dance in a tent with only an oil lamp for light. One day they went to lunch at Elmenteita with Lord Delamere, whom they had not met before; they both liked him very much. My father wrote: 'He . . . has done more for this country than anyone. . . . He is a man who has the good of the country at heart and does not try and profiteer himself.' He had in fact acquired a hundred thousand acres from the Government and was dividing it up into what he thought would be economic holdings of two or three thousand acres each for new settlers. Much of it was waterless and so he put in a pipeline across the plains, taking water from a river high up in the forest behind Njoro. His land went from there down the Molo river as far as Kampi-ya-Moto, the Hot Camp, so called as it had been one of the camping places on the route for the foot safaris going up to Uganda.

It was not known at that time that much of this land had a cobalt deficiency and cattle wasted away if left to graze on it too long at a time. That and the fact that there was no water on most of it was the reason the Masai had not used this land in the past. Once the cobalt deficiency was discovered, cobalt was put into the water and when the cattle drank it would pass through their systems into the dung and would leach into the ground. Now that land is some of the best cattle land in the country.

They went racing at Nakuru where my mother was astonished to find the ladies suddenly wearing smart clothes. They also went to Naivasha, visited the Government farm, which was being managed by a man called Armstrong from the Borders, and went duck shooting on the lake early in the morning. My mother says: 'It was so beautiful, with the whole world turning to gold as the sun got up and the numerous lovely birds that were flying all around.' The duck shooting was not too successful as they could not find the boat in the dark and then it kept getting stuck in the papyrus. They went out shooting at Njoro without much success either, but said that there was an abundance of game and they were warned not to ride too far as there were many lions about, no one having shot them during the war. They also visited the Clutterbucks' racing stables nearby to see if they could find any horses to suit them. Staying at the same place was Brigadier-General Sladen CB, CMG, DSO, MC. He had been in the Rifle Brigade and had had a brilliant career during the war. He had served before that in 1906 in the King's African Rifles in East Africa and in the Somali Camel Corps from 1908 to 1910. He, like my father, had been allotted a soldier-settler farm in North Kenya but had not taken it up. His wife was a beautiful Scottish girl, Mabel Orr-Ewing, from Cardross near Stirling. They had just bought some land on the Molo River and my parents decided to go and see it with the idea that they might buy some land nearby. The price being asked was £3. 7s. 6d per acre in sterling with thirty years to pay and 8 per cent interest on the unpaid amount. They planned to grow flax, which at that time was supposed to have a wonderful future. They had some difficulty getting to the Sladens' camp on the farm, as there were no roads and two rivers to cross with no bridges and my mother expected the little car to be smashed to atoms. But they got there in the end, found the Sladens having an excellent lunch from a Fortnum and Mason chop box and were able to pitch their camp not far off.

My mother or the African driver always did the driving as to his dying day my father never learned to drive a car. Having been shot through the sciatic nerve he had no feeling in his bad leg, which may have been a deterrent; but many people with artificial legs are able to drive, even without hand controls, and I suspect my father could have driven if he had tried. But like most of our family, he had an aversion to anything mechanical.

On that first night they had an early dinner by a huge camp fire. My mother writes:

> It was delightfully cool and fresh. I sat in my fur coat with a heavenly smell of burning wood round me from our own fire, besides that of our cook and servants, and another one for the syces and outside boys. It reminded me of camp fires in Canada. The stars were beautiful . . . Twice during the night we heard strange sounds which sounded like a cross between a mule and a horse. I thought it must be a zebra but the boys said it was a lion . . .

The farm that they were attracted by and hoped to buy was on the western edge of the Great Rift Valley, a few miles south of the Equator. It lay between 6,000 and 7,000 feet above sea level.

The next day when exploring they saw swarms of game: kongoni, ostrich, steenbok, Thomson's gazelle, koraan and herds and herds of zebra. They got up early and mounted on ponies, followed by one boy carrying the rifles and another carrying the Kodak, thermos and sandwich case, they went up through some attractive jungly forest, but could find no path until they came upon some native huts where a charming Kikuyu young man offered himself as a guide. He sprang from stone to stone and 'it was a pleasure to watch his beautiful, athletic body'. He took them right to the boundary of the farm at the top of the hill. 'The air was glorious' and there were many of the 'Red Lily trees' (erythrina) flaming crimson in the sun. They worked their way down looking for a house site, and found a nice place, but not so good as the Sladens' since it was so far from water (the Sladens' house had five springs). My mother said that she was consumed with jealousy. 'But we must not grudge the Sladens their nice site as they are such charming people and we shall be lucky to have them as neighbours, especially as their children are the same ages as ours.' My father describes the land as follows:

The River Molo flows at the foot of the ground, and even at this time, the driest time of the year, there is plenty of water in it for all our needs. The lowest land is 6,300 feet and it goes up several hundred feet until the back part is on the top of the mountain almost. The soil for the most part is excellent, in fact very rich indeed, of a sort of dark chocolate loam. There is a large extent that could be cleared and put under flax at once. Then the ground gently rises for about two miles back with some parts thickly wooded. This goes on till one comes to the steep hills behind. The Sladens' land is more hilly than ours and not quite so easily cleared for cultivation, but they have an ideal site for a house with little streams flowing on both sides while their house will be surrounded by big trees, chiefly flat topped thorns. We have found an equally attractive spot for our house except there is no water and we should have to get water from the river about two and a half miles away. It would be quite easy to make a road as the ground is on a very gentle gradient and I expect one could lay on water by pipe, but that requires going into more carefully. We have water on our land in the form of swamps formed by the streams on the Sladens' land and they will be very useful to us, but they are some way from the proposed site for a house. It is very difficult to decide and it takes a long time to get over the land as at the moment we only have one very indifferent pony which is lent to us . . . If I decide to buy, Sladen and I are going to work together this year to try and get one hundred and fifty acres on our joint boundary under flax. In this way we should get a return the first year. I think I shall buy, but must make a few more enquiries about water . . . We have had three very happy days in our small tent with our few native servants. The mornings and evenings are perfect, but the sun is hot in the middle of the day. We go to bed at nine and get up at six and rest a bit in the heat of the day. It is a fine life and makes one feel fit and well. We have seen a certain amount of game, zebra, hartebests, reedbuck, pig, guinea fowl, and Khoraan and heard a lion one night and have seen the spoor of buffalo and rhino. Another advantage to this land is that it will be near a railway when the Uasin Gishu line is built.

Like General Sladen, my father had a soldier-settler farm allotted him. This was on the Laikipia Plains in the north of Kenya and although they had pretty well decided that it was too remote and that they would not want to live there, they thought that they had better go to see it. Perhaps they could run it with a manager or go into partnership with a neighbour. They started off by staying two nights at Santamor with Mervyn Ridley, and my mother practised riding astride. She had always ridden side-saddle before but she managed quite well. They set off for Naromoru via Nyeri. The road was very narrow, twisty and precipitous, and they had been warned to look out for Lord Carbery who had a habit of driving a lorry full pelt down the road, giving way to nobody. Their car was loaded to the roof with luggage and contained two Africans as well as themselves. Before long the foot brake gave out, and my mother found it difficult to negotiate the bends and hills with only the handbrake; meanwhile my father blew the horn in case Lord Carbery was anywhere near. Luckily they came upon him stopped at a river putting water into his lorry. Having reached Nyeri for lunch and having got the brake repaired they went on to Berkeley Cole's place at Solio. My mother says:

We have got a rather dirty little wooden room with a very suspicious looking bed which I sprinkled freely with Keatings, and a glorious big bath. I was inches deep in red sand and it was a great luxury to lie and soak as long as I liked, having mercifully brought my own bath towel. It is the fashion in this country to dine in pyjamas and dressingown which takes a little getting used to. I can't describe how curious Mr Cole appeared as he slouched into the drawingroom in a very old pair of slippers and what looked like shrunken crepe drawers and an old bed jacket. It certainly was not long enough to make any pretence of hiding his naked legs. I was startled and Francis thought I would have hysterics. However, Mr Cole was quite unmoved and made no allusion to his strange attire. During dinner a large cat wandered all over the table and a huge Russian boarhound, a magnificent animal, ate off our plates at will.

She says next morning that many animals roamed in and out of the house; three sheep came in at luncheon and hens pecked around the table. All the same, she thought Mr Cole was one of the most amusing men she had ever met. Berkeley and his brother Galbraith Cole, famously free-spirited sons of the 4th Earl of Enniskillen, were later immortalized in Karen Blixen's *Out of Africa*.

They had engaged forty Kavirondo porters and set off to camp on the soldier-settler farm – a difficult journey as they had to cross the Uasin Nyiro and Burguret rivers and had to walk for some time through long grass with no track. Both my parents tried to shoot meat for the porters, but my father had to ride a white pony as he could not walk much and that made stalking difficult (my mother prayed he would not try to shoot a lion from the pony!). They did however manage to shoot one or two reed buck. At night it was difficult to sleep as the ponies had to be tied very near the tents because of the lions and they stamped and sneezed continually; also the zebra made a 'deafening noise' all night. The camp fire was kept alight.

They visited some South African Boer farmers who lived nearby and were very impressed by their fruit and vegetable garden; my mother was pleased, too, to see how well the children looked. They were given a large bowl of strawberries and cream and some plum cake. But by now they had definitely decided that they did not want the soldier-settler farm and eventually it was sold to someone else. Moreover, they had heard that the sale of the farm on the Molo river had gone through. So now they were committed; they were to be Kenya settlers for the rest of their lives.

5
Making a Start

All this time Moy and I were in England, mostly at Minto in our grandmother's charge. My parents agreed that my mother should go to fetch us while my father stayed in Africa to get things started on the farm. That is how I came to think he had turned black! But it was some time before this was all settled and meanwhile my parents encountered two of the problems which were always cropping up in Kenya in colonial days – the question of 'forced labour' and relations between settlers and officials. They got rid of their porters and camping outfit and went to stay at Embu with my mother's cousin, Jock Elliot, who was District Commissioner there, in charge of administering the natives.

They reached Embu in the afternoon – a nice house with comfortable chairs, good books and pictures. According to my mother, 'There was a lovely garden and a grass tennis court and a very smart guard with sentries – great big men with beautiful figures.' While resting before dinner, she was horrified to see a large rat playing about in her room. When she mentioned this to Jock, he did not seem at all surprised and his only comment was to advise her to sleep with the lantern under the bed. My mother wrote that Jock looked very smart in his uniform, my father that he was very nice and gave them a very good dinner but that he had a bee in his bonnet on the subject of labour. My father says:

It is a very acute question, as if this country is to progress it must have more labour, but the natives won't come out to work but prefer to remain in the native reserves and watch their women work. They require very little to live on, so do not need to make money outside. The settlers, of course, keep clamouring for the Government to provide more labour, but the question is, how to get it? One then comes to the question of 'forced labour' so called. That is to say each chief is required to provide so many men from their tribe to go out to work for the settlers, and if they don't they are liable to fines and other punishments. Now it is illegal to force out labour, but the Governor, Northey, issued instructions that the local officers were to do so. Jock refuses to do this, and says he may have to resign over it. He feels very strongly about it but takes a very pro-native point of view. It is a very difficult problem, but if the country is to be developed it must have labour. How to obtain it is beyond me, as I do not know enough of the conditions; but something must be done. I had a slight argument with Jock last night, but he got so excited at once that I dropped the subject . . . We came all through a large native reserve yesterday, all the way from Nyeri the most beautiful soil I have ever seen, which would grow coffee and everything but is very slightly cultivated by the natives, a few patches of sweet potatoes, etc., just enough for their own needs. Personally, I rather feel that since old Ham laughed at his father Noah for getting drunk, all his descendants have been meant to serve the descendants of Japheth! But perhaps I am selfishly thinking of my own future flax crops, etc.

This question of natives being forced out to work for the settlers has been held against them ever since. Now of course the problem is *un*employment. It was a very difficult question because if there were to be settlers and they were to buy land and develop it they had to have labour. To the Africans, the idea of one man working for another was something they had never experienced. Of course they had done communal work, when building houses or clearing land and so on. But in that case one man would work for another one day and everyone would work for him the next. There was nothing like paid labour. They saw no reason why they should work for these strange 'Wazungu' who had come uninvited to their country. When the Government imposed 'hut tax', which meant that the head of the family had to pay so much for each hut in his compound, Africans had to raise some money to pay it, but they could usually do this by selling some stock or produce. Only if this was not possible did they go out to work. This labour problem went on for some years, but as a general rule the good employers did not have much trouble in getting labour. There were always a few young men who wanted to see the world and try a new kind of life away from home, or perhaps they wanted to move off because of some quarrel, or perhaps someone was trying to bewitch them. It was the bad employers, who could not manage their labour well, who were always short and rushing to the Government to get them some men.

A. C. Hoey – a very early settler – once told me how, long ago, before the First World War, he had grown some maize in the foothills of the Cherangani Mountains and some Marakwet young men had come and helped him harvest it. When they had finished he gave them each two shillings. They looked at these coins doubtfully and then handed them back saying: 'We don't know what is the use of these things, and we did not expect payment, we only came to help you because you are our neighbour. But if you really want to give us something, we would be very grateful for some matches.'

The next morning my parents witnessed Jock deposing a 'Paramount Chief'. He had apparently been misbehaving himself for some time. My mother says:

It was a most picturesque ceremony. Jock was seated in a chair with his Assistant District Commissioner beside him, a very smart Guard of the Kings African Rifles behind him; in front of him, squatting on the grass, were hundreds of natives, some of them clad in beads and skins, some in brightly-hued blankets, most of them with lions' manes on their heads, others with curious little hats made of clipped vulture feathers, all armed with assegais, the point of which was covered with a large black Pompom made of ostrich feathers which signifies 'We come in peace'. Jock spoke in Swahili which was translated to the different tribes by an interpreter. After speaking gravely for some time, Jock ordered the Sergeant of the Guard to remove the gold-hilted stick from the Chief. It is marvellous that two white men sitting alone and unarmed amongst a crowd of savages can achieve this quite peaceably. The Chief had a very clever face with good, well-cut features; he is said to be a very clever man. Jock expects things to go smoothly for a few weeks but there will be so much intrigue that trouble is sure to occur sooner or later.

My father added, 'It does really show the superiority of the white man; we are a wonderful nation.'

What my parents didn't understand was that traditionally the Embu do not have chiefs. They are ruled by the old men in the elders' age group. This so-called 'Chief' may or may not have been someone that they respected. Sometimes a cunning man would ingratiate himself with the British Government for his own ends and this may have been the case here. He was certainly appointed by the Government. Also, could one really say 'two unarmed white men were sitting alone amongst hundreds of armed savages' when there was a fully armed guard of King's African Rifles present?

My mother 'didn't think Jock was very popular – with the Europeans, I suppose she meant. Although the officials and settlers came from the same race, and mostly from the same backgrounds, there was a gulf between them. The settlers did not take kindly to rules and regulations and red tape. They were usually individualists or they would not have been where they were. They had for the most part put everything they possessed into the country and were hoping to spend the rest of their lives there and pass on what they had when they died to their children.

Officials, on the other hand, were the paid servants of the Government who had to carry out orders from Whitehall which often seemed remote from local problems. They were posted to a district and before long moved to another – and they would eventually retire to Britain. So it was inevitable that they should look at things from a different angle. Not surprisingly, most officials would rather be posted to a native reserve, where they were lords of all they surveyed, than to areas with settlers who challenged every new regulation that they didn't like. Some of the more rabid settlers would even refuse to meet officials socially. Later on the laws were changed so that officials could buy land and become settlers and some of the settlers' sons even became officials.

My parents had not taken Loder on this trip to the North but my mother says:

My boy, Mahindi is the most excellent maid and I always find my sunburn lotion, sponges, cold cream and clean vest put ready for me before there seems to have been time to unload the car. He never unpacks unnecessary things, but always has the exact things that I want, like my comfortable shoes ready for me when I come in tired, so unlike a maid who unpacks so much more but always leaves the things one longs for most at the bottom of the box and one has to pretend not to want them.

On 24 March 1920, after a few days in Nairobi, they drove to their camp on the farm – which was now theirs. They had found a nice site near a spring, near where our tennis court was later, and my mother writes:

It took quite a long time loading up the car with all our various baggage, rifles, luncheon baskets all piled round Loder, whose head just emerged over the top of it all. She is still dressed in her dusty blue serge and looks most incongruous, but is quite splendid and minds nothing. We only just got the tents pitched before dark and had a rather uncomfortable time as none of our pots and pans had arrived nor Loder's bed. However, Francis did not mind sleeping on the ground and the cook did marvels with one saucepan which he happened to have, and two plates from the luncheon basket. I wish I could have taken a Kodak of Loder arriving in the camp this afternoon. She was preceded by a long line of coal black porters quite naked except for a scarlet blanket flung over a very small portion of their anatomies, coloured bead necklaces, their ears distorted by endless coils of wire, or bits of wood, safety pins or huge brass hooks. They stretch their ears to such an extent that a ring of flesh hangs down several inches. They each balanced some very small package on their heads and trudged solemnly along, Loder bringing up the rear with her battered topi on the back of her head.

My father and General Sladen had decided to pool their resources and try to get 150 to 300 acres of flax planted that year, quite a task, as the land had still to be cleared of bush. They took on a 'Dutchman' (an Afrikaner) and bought 112 young oxen which he was to train. They also bought four ploughs, two wagons and two harrows. They also had forty labourers. The Dutchman had his wife and children with him and my father says that he is 'not a bad fellow but like all Boers hard to get a move on'. They also took on a chauffeur, cook and two houseboys. The cook was a Muganda, (that is, from Uganda) and my mother says most excellent, and she hopes he will be as good in a kitchen as he is in a hole in the ground. He is paid Rs.45 and she says most other people pay Goan cooks twice that amount. A source of anxiety is that their house site will be too near the Sladens'; they are only about 400 yards apart and my father says it seems rather stupid to live in a semi-detached villa in the middle of an African forest. But the site is much the nicest they have found and as there are a lot of trees between them, they hope it will not matter. My mother is already visualizing her garden with lawns and terraces and beautiful trees. Meanwhile they have bought two ponies for £90 and £60. My mother's habit of putting up a sunshade while riding could frighten a pony; and one of them kicked my father quite badly on his leg and laid him up for a short time.

My mother never forgot the beauty of her last morning in camp.

The sun rises about six, I woke soon afterwards, and watched the changing loveliness from my bed. It was perfectly still, very thick dew glistening on the grass and a golden haze in the distance, like a fine September morning at home, our fire still alight and every now and then a puff of delicious smelling smoke wafted into the tent, the birds singing everywhere. The colouring of the butterflies and birds are amazing – brilliant greens and blues and crimsons.

On the way to Nairobi they stayed at KeKopey, near Gilgil with Galbraith and Nell Cole. He and Berkeley Cole were brothers-in-law of Lord Delamere, whose first wife, Florence, had been their sister. Nell was the niece of Arthur Balfour, the Prime Minister. Poor Galbraith was badly crippled by arthritis. My mother says Nell was 'a nice woman but so unsoignée, and not our type [my mother always pronounced it "teep"] in the least; very Balfourish and I should think very clever . . .'

On 20 April 1920 my mother and Loder boarded their ship and my father went back to Nairobi, where he found that the farm had been finally valued at £3. 2. 6d. per acre. He went back to his camp on the farm and started to live the life of a farmer. Although he had been brought up in the country, his interests had all been to do with sport and he had never done a day's farming in his life. Nor had General Sladen. Both were full of optimism and enthusiasm but problems soon began to emerge. They had to sack the Dutchman as he was 'useless for anything but training the oxen'. They bought a Titan tractor and engaged a Eurasian driver. They were kept very busy as everything had to be supervised personally and it was frustrating not to know enough of the language to make themselves understood. My father bought four milk cows for £17. 10s. each and made a start on the house. He found some suitable stone for building and took on an Indian *mistri* (skilled workman) and twenty-five labourers. The name of the architect was Henderson.

The two of them went to Njoro for a meeting about building a flax factory there, and another day my father went to a mass meeting of the farmers of the district to discuss labour problems. 'Delamere was in the chair. No decisions were come to but two telegrams – badly worded, I thought, but didn't like to say – were sent home re exchange and other matters. I was not much struck with the settlers' powers of argument but Delamere was an excellent Chairman.'

They managed to get about 160 acres of flax planted, but had continual worries over it. The first germination was bad: the seed was poor and the rains intermittent. Then caterpillars came and devoured much of what did germinate; my father says sadly that he would reap little that year but experience. The Eurasian disappeared, so the tractor had to be driven either by my father's driver or by General Sladen. It was very difficult to get it started but my father says he managed it with the aid of the 'book of words', even though he was a fool at mechanics and had never driven anything in his life. General Sladen was much better at starting it. They had continual problems in getting fuel, which had to come on the railway – described as 'very unreliable being run by the Government'.

My father had to attend some meetings with the local farmers from time to time and they often asked him to take the chair. 'This, one might think a compliment, as I was such a newcomer, but it was really because I had been out too short a time to have quarrelled with anyone yet!'

There was one meeting in Nakuru to protest about the railway line being altered. It had been decided long ago to have a line up to the Uasin Gishu, and the line as surveyed was to go from Nakuru to Eldoret. The Government had announced that this was the route, and had issued maps with the line shown and even the positions and names of the stations. There was to be a station three miles from our farm, to be called the Molo River station. Then the contractor engineer came out and reported that if the line were taken from another point it could be built quicker and would save £4,000,000, with which he could build a branch line forty miles long to serve all our part of the country and still save half a million pounds to be devoted to the Thika railway extension. This was accordingly agreed in Legislative Council.

The meeting was to ask for the immediate construction of the branch line, which having eighty miles already surveyed could be put in hand at once. My father was put in the chair but Delamere had to do all the talking as he was member for the district in the Legislative Council. The meeting was very amicable.

My father went to some dances in Nakuru and met the doctor's wife Tissie and her friend Tossie. They were both Gaiety Girls on the London stage, and referred to the doctor as 'our husband'. They did not like Nakuru and were longing to get back to London.

My mother was away for nearly a year, collecting us children and buying things we should need. During that time my father got to know some of his neighbours and went to Nairobi for the first of his race weeks, the great social events of the year, when farmers came together from all over the colony. These happened in July and January, and in Nairobi he was able to play cricket, bridge and even squash, in spite of his leg. There were dinners and dances as well as the races; he went to an Old Etonian dinner as well as one for Grenadiers – officers and other ranks; he got to know the Governor and his wife and had talks about the future of the country. And of course there was the racing; he became a Steward of the Jockey Club and knew most of the trainers.

So 1920 came to an end. It had been a momentous year for my parents. They had come to Africa as strangers, and within two months they had sunk most of their small capital in three thousand odd acres of virgin land that had never been farmed before, except for Masai grazing. They had started to clear the bush, to plough and plant crops and to build themselves a large house. They had entered into the social life with gusto and had been drawn into the political and sporting life of the colony.

PART II
Growing Up

1

The House Is Built

The big house was being built and making progress slowly. The men building it were Indians of different kinds. Some of them used to wear little caps with pigtails hanging down behind. I asked my father why they had these pigtails and he told me that they believed that when they died God would pull them up to Heaven with them. We had great fun as children playing about in the building when it was being put up and climbing up and down the scaffolding. At some time in 1922 it was ready to be lived in and very spiendid it was. It had two storeys and was built in pinky-brown stone with a Mangalore tiled roof. It had two verandahs, one on the upper floor and one on the ground floor, with arches. The rooms were spacious and had high ceilings and the roof had large overhangs because at that time people always wanted to keep out of the sun. The floors were of cedar which had been sawn on the farm, and there were big beams of *podo* (podo carpas) to support the upper floor. My parents had brought furniture from their house in London, all of which had been brought to the farm in ox wagons from Njoro railway station, twenty miles away. On the ground floor we had a drawing-room, a dining-room, a hall with a big wooden staircase to the upstairs, a sitting-room for my mother and one for my father, and a large spare bedroom with dressing-room and bathroom. Upstairs there was my parents' bedroom, dressing-room and bathroom, our night nursery, day nursery and bathroom and a bedroom for Loder.

In my parents' room there was black and gold Italian furniture, and the drawing-room and dining-room too were furnished from their London house. In our nurseries and the spare room the local *fundis* (workmen) had made plain unvarnished cedar furniture. There were cretonne covers on the chairs and curtains. In the drawing-room there was a large stone fireplace which had been designed by my grandmother, Mary Minto.

We had quite a large household. There was Ero, my father's personal boy; my mother and Loder each had their personal boy and we had our nursery boy. There was a headboy, a cook and kitchen *toto* and a pantry boy as well as outside staff such as gardeners, drivers, syces and so on. I use the expression 'boy' or 'personal boy' because that is what we used to call them. Nowadays it is thought derogatory to call people 'boys' when they are grown men and I understand this, because most Africans pass through their initiation into their tribe from being a boy to manhood. But I don't think any of us thought it insulting; it was like the French for waiter. A *toto*, though, really was a boy. All these people in our household were ruled over by Loder with a rod of iron. They used to call her 'Gateru' which means 'beard' because of her somewhat wispy chin. She used to keep them up to the mark all the time and tried to train them to be like the servants she had known in England in the 'best 'ouses'. She used to scream at them in a torrent of Cockney abuse. We heard shouts of, 'Oo do you think you are, you great big bamboo? A gentleman?' When she said 'You great big bamboo', she meant '*Bumbafu*' which is Swahili for 'fool'. My father always said that he expected any day to see the cook come rushing in with a chopper dripping blood, saying he could stand this abuse no longer. But in fact they were really quite fond of her because she used to look after them very well. She was forever making them cups of tea, giving them medicine when they were ill and so on. One day she appeared in my mother's room and said: 'Oo m'lady, the boy is killing the cook with a knife, the blood is pouring. 'E says 'e'll take an axe to 'im.' So my mother had to go out and bind up their wounds and forbid any more fighting. Loder must have lived a lonely life because she always ate alone and sat in her own room. She never came to our rooms except when she was working. She used sometimes to come to my father when he was working in his office and say 'Is it true, m'lord?' and he would say 'Is what true, Loder?' 'What they say in the papers, m'lord.' 'No, Loder,' he would reply, 'never believe anything you read in the papers.' She was a first-class cook and a very economical housekeeper and woe betide anyone who overcharged on anything. Her greatest pleasure was to go shopping in Nakuru and bargain with the shopkeepers. My father said he thought a day shopping in Nakuru gave her as much pleasure as a game of polo gave him.

Loder had a little dachshund dog called Tim. She would hug him and croon endearments to him in baby talk – 'Tim's Mama's little darling baby boy' and so on. My father used to say: 'Disgusting! Fancy talking to a dog like that!'

Many people at that time had Somali upper servants, as very few of the local Africans were trained. But as we had Loder this was unnecessary and we only had the local people. Most of the superior servants or people in responsible positions were, in those days, Moslems; either Somalis or coast Africans. House servants always wore the Moslem dress, a *kanzu*, which is a long kind of shirt down to the ground, and either an embroidered cotton cap or a red fez. Our servants always wore these clothes waiting at table. They would wear tussore silk *kanzus* with rose-coloured waistcoats made of brocade with silver bindings, and very smart they looked. They kept to the Moslem custom of always covering their heads and coming into the house barefoot. If it hadn't been for their religion, Moslems would have played a much bigger part in Kenya; but as all the schools in the early days were run by missionaries, who of course hoped their pupils would become Christians, the Moslems wouldn't send their children to them and therefore lagged behind in education and were overtaken by the mission-educated up-country people, often Kikuyu.

My parents had to think of a name for the house and farm. They could find no local African name, so they decided to call it 'Deloraine' after the knight, William of Deloraine in Sir Walter Scott's poem 'The Lay of the Last Minstrel'. Deloraine is in fact a place in Selkirkshire on the borders of England and Scotland, and provided the title, now extinct, originally bestowed on a younger son of the Duke of Monmouth and Anne Scott, Duchess of Buccleuch. Sir Walter Scott pronounced it 'Dellorain' but in Scotland they pronounce it 'De-lorrin'. It is said to come from the Gaelic 'Dal Orein' which means 'Orein's land', Orein being a Celtic saint. Others say it is 'de la reine'. In any case, the house and farm have been called Deloraine ever since. It is not a very good name for this country as many Africans cannot pronounce 'l's and 'r's very well and so the name gets corrupted.

Once we had got established in our new house we started having visitors of all kinds. One of our earliest visitors was my mother's sister, Ruby Cromer. In 1921 her husband, Rowland Cromer, had to go with the Prince of Wales when he did his tour of India; so my Aunt Ruby came and stayed with us during part of that time. He later joined her. My father's niece Mida Scott also came for a while and later her sister, Mary, who eventually married David Burghley, the Olympic hurdler, later Marquess of Exeter.

One night my parents gave a dance and my mother describes the party as follows:

Last night we had our first real party and put two people into each of the four huts. We had been lent tents and some extra beds . . . we sat down sixteen at dinner, which was a great effort on mine and Loder's part. She really did very well. The silver was clean and the whole timing went well. Lord Delamere, who sat next to me kept saying: 'I don't know how it could be done in Africa.' We had had a drought for two months, no rain at all; but on this night we had a heavy deluge which ruined all the lovely lanterns that Freddie Ward had spent the whole morning putting up – but in spite of the weather nearly everyone turned up; I suppose between fifty and sixty people. They danced to the gramophone till four thirty a.m. I thought I should drop, I could hardly stand on my poor tired feet to say goodnight. However, I am glad it was a success. But it is entirely due to Loder, who produced excellent consommé for all the guests at supper, chaud-froid of chicken, excellent pastry and cream. The drinks were the weak spot, I thought, as we only gave cider cup; wine would have made it too expensive, so everyone had to drink this or whiskey or beer.

In 1924 we had the Duke and Duchess of York (later King George VI and Queen Elizabeth) to stay and I remember there was great excitement while preparing the house for them and their rather large party. Lord Delamere was one of them. They stayed two days and played polo and went racing and in due course departed to go to Uganda. However, just as they left, the Governor at that time – Sir Robert Coryndon – died and so there was a change of plan. My father and the Duke of York had to go to Nairobi to attend the funeral but the Duchess of York – now the Queen Mother – came back here. My mother was in a terrible state as the large party had just left and all the sheets were in the wash and the food all finished. The Duke and Duchess were in the Governor's train and it stopped at Rongai to let her out but there was no one to meet her except someone who just happened to be there in a rather dilapidated old box-body car which had no doors. (Box-body cars were all shapes and sizes, being home-made on an imported chassis.) The Duchess was pushed into the car over where the door should have been and driven back here. The thing I remember chiefly about her visit was that she used to ride my pony every day which upset me somewhat since it meant that I couldn't ride myself. But she only stayed a few days.

Later my parents built a mud and wattle cottage adjacent to the main house with three rooms and a bathroom in it. Loder used one of these as her sitting-room and the others were kept for guests. We also had the four original huts so we could accommodate quite a number of people.

It was a joy for my mother when my grandmother, Mary Minto, came to stay in 1925. My grandmother took everything in her stride and enjoyed herself immensely. They did a safari to Uganda together and in Kampala they went to see the grave of Raymond Portal who died of fever there in 1893. He and his brother Sir Gerald, who died a year later and was the first British Commissioner to Uganda, were first cousins of my Minto grandfather. They were largely responsible for persuading the British Parliament to lay claim to the entire territory. The Uganda town of Fort Portal still bears their name.

In 1928 the Prince of Wales stayed and he rode one of my father's horses in the Nakuru races. We also had a number of politicians to stay when they came out on various commissions like the Hilton Young Commission and the Carter Commission, which looked into land and education. People from all walks of life stayed with us. One day my mother tells how Loder rushed into her sitting-room and said 'Oo m'lady, 'is lordship's got a tramp in the 'ouse.' My mother went out to see who it was and found one of our neighbours who had been on safari and who was very dirty and unshaven. His shirt looked as though he hadn't washed it for a couple of months and he was covered with veldt sores on which the flies kept settling. My father had been out riding and had met him and thought he looked hungry so he brought him in for a good square meal.

My mother had by this time settled down to life on an African farm. She always used to wear her pearls and her earrings; her hands were always covered with rings and she used to wear beige-fawn gloves, a bush jacket type of shirt with riding breeches and mosquito boots. These boots were made out of light suede, like riding boots. She always carried a sunshade as well as wearing her hat when she was out of doors.

She longed to have a beautiful garden, and had visions of rose-covered pergolas, lawns and terraces and herbaceous borders filled with bright flowering annuals such as she knew at 'home'. Unfortunately, there was never enough water for the plants and so whenever the dry weather set in, most of them withered away and she became very disheartened. In those days people didn't know of the many attractive drought-resistant trees and shrubs that are available now for hot, dry areas. But as we lived at the edge of the forest there were some lovely indigenous trees in our garden such as sugonoior greenheart (*Warburgia ugandensis*) and morijo (*Acacanthera schimperii*), which is the arrow poison tree. When boiled up the roots produce a black sticky substance that was put on the tips of arrows for hunting; when it entered the bloodstream it caused a quick death. My parents called these trees olives, but in fact they had nothing to do with olives, though there were some other trees of the olive family in the forest.

My mother loved going to dances, though the circumstances were often very trying. Once someone gave her a lift in the kind of car most settlers had, what is now called a pick-up. She was sitting in a chair on the open platform at the back when they went over a big bump and she found herself sitting on her chair in the middle of the road, rather dazed. When the driver discovered she wasn't there he went back – to find she had been picked up by the next car. She was worried by headaches for a few weeks after that.

We had problems with water and for many years, until a borehole was sunk near the house, all the water had to be fetched up in an ox-drawn cart from the river, two miles away, and tipped into an underground tank at the rear of the house from which it was then pumped up by hand to the storage tank in the roof.

Besides playing polo at Njoro on Sundays, my parents would go out visiting some of their neighbours. The Grants, Jos and Nellie, the parents of Elspeth Huxley, who had been at Thika, had moved up to Njoro. One day my parents went up in the car to have lunch with them and on the way back one of the car's wheels caught in a rut and the car toppled over, turning completely upside down. It hadn't been going very well before this but after it had turned upside down it went much better. Very often, my mother says, they had to finish their journeys on foot for one reason or another.

In those days when we were still small, my parents managed to get about a good deal and see a good many people. Once they went to the house of Karen Blixen, who wrote *Out of Africa*. She was in Europe and had lent it to Denys Finch-Hatton (Karen's lover), who was their host. My mother describes him as 'one of the most attractive personalities I know, so charming and well-read and delightful in every way. But one hardly ever sees him because he is a wanderer, perpetually in the blue.' On another occasion she describes a peaceful day in idyllic surroundings near Mount Kenya:

> It was so cool and peaceful sitting by the water with only the tinkling of the cattle and goat bells . . . While Sybil and I were having lunch under a large fig tree, we suddenly saw a magnificent figure approaching. A tall naked man with many bronze and bead ornaments. A little clipped close-fitting hat of black ostrich feathers on his head and one gigantically tall snow white ostrich feather in front, his whole body glistening with oil and red mud. He was preceded by two tall magnificent men carrying spears tipped with black ostrich pompoms. He was followed by two more men entirely covered in red mud and looking like red Greek statues . . . He was the Sultani of the district and he was going to dispense justice . . .

Her letters are full of contrasts: the car breaks down miles from anywhere but they are saved by a kind young doctor who gives them a wonderful dinner; they spend the night in the house of the Assistant District

Commissioner, who is away on tour – but there is not a stick of furniture and everything is swarming with ants. 'The horror of getting up!' she writes. 'Everything, stockings, slippers, one mass of those vile ants!'

My father had taken some shares in racehorses. They were being trained at Njoro by Mr Clutterbuck's daughter, then Beryl Purves. She had married Purves when she was only sixteen. The story was that her father had reckoned her age like a racehorse from 1 August (as all thoroughbreds were aged in Kenya) and thought that she was seventeen. Later she married again and as Beryl Markham became famous for being the first person to fly solo across the Atlantic from east to west. One day my parents set off to see these horses, but the car refused to go up the hill and they had to walk the last part of the journey.

When my father was away the manager of the farm used to come and see my mother every evening. One day he shocked her by saying: 'What shall I do with the bodies?' 'What bodies?' she asked in horror. 'They are hanging from a tree,' he replied. Apparently two women and a child had been killed. It was something to do with witchcraft and their bodies had been hung in a tree 'to make more medicine'. My mother didn't want to interfere with the magic and told him to leave the bodies till the police arrived. 'A very nice policeman soon arrived.' He seemed more preoccupied with the English look of the house and its furniture than with the murder. He had only been two months in the police and didn't know much of any language; however, he went off to investigate through an interpreter. It soon emerged that the murderers were Kikuyu and the other Kikuyu soon gave them away. A hundred bottles of 'magic powder' were brought to the manager's hut and the main culprits taken to prison. It must have been difficult for the early settlers dealing with such things, when they had so little knowledge of the people and their customs.

My father became rather depressed about the farm because we had so many droughts and the price of everything had fallen so much. My mother sometimes became homesick and she writes:

> Sometimes I wonder whether it is a great waste of life living out here and being a drudge and meeting no-one except delightful farmers. Then I order a pony and gallop up the hill in the sunshine and stand at the top gazing over the limitless spaces of Africa with the glorious wind blowing the delicious Mimosa scent against my face and wonder if I haven't got the best kind of life possible after all.

My father had also invested in some land between Deloraine and Nakuru, near Menengai Crater. We called it the 'Pipeline' because it is where Lord Delamere had put in a pipeline to enable people to farm in that area, which had previously had no water. The work oxen had to be changed backwards and forwards between Deloraine and Menengai because if they stayed too long at Menengai they became thin as a result of the cobalt deficiency and so had to be returned to Deloraine to be fattened up again. Farms in this area were also unsuccessful because they were mainly for growing maize and were severely plagued by locusts. Anyone who has not seen a swarm of locusts cannot imagine what terrible insects they are. They come in their millions and settle on the maize and just chew, chew, chew as fast as they can eat, and what goes in comes out again from their other end. You can hear them chewing and in half an hour or so you have no maize left, just stalks sticking up and your whole crop is ruined. That is bad enough for large-scale farmers who have invested a lot of money in their crop, but it is far worse for the peasant farmer whose crop is his whole food supply for the next year. As children we would go out with everyone else and beat tins with sticks trying to get them to move away but it didn't make much difference.

Locusts can only fly in certain temperatures, so they cannot fly at night, early morning or evening. They have to settle during these times and the Africans went about with sacks filling them up with locusts. They then roasted the insects and ate them. The only good thing that you can say about a locust is that at least you can eat it.

The locusts used to come to East Africa from Arabia where they bred in the desert. Nowadays there is an organization called the Desert Locust Control, who go to all the breeding places, find the hoppers – young locusts – as they come out of the holes where the eggs had been laid, and destroy them. This has made a tremendous difference to farming in Kenya.

After a few years my father sold these Menengai pipeline farms and lost money over that too. He also invested in a gold mine at Kakamega in north-west Kenya. During the early Thirties gold was found in small quantities at Kakamega, first of all by panning the rivers and later by mining, but not enough to pay; I don't think that he ever got anything out of his mine and eventually it was abandoned.

2
Growing Up

Meanwhile, on the farm Moy and I were growing up. We used to run around in khaki shirts and shorts, barefooted most of the time. We liked to get our feet really hard so that we could run over the rough ground, stones and thorny places without feeling uncomfortable. We were mostly in the company of the Sladen girls – Eddie had gone home to school – and our ponies were the chief joy of our lives; we rode most evenings with the syces. After Noor Khan died, he was replaced by a young man, Mohammed Khan. He came to the farm with his wife who was in purdah. They lived in a little mud and thatched house with a fenced-in yard behind their kitchen and his wife never ventured out. In fact, I never saw her; we were told never to go in to look at her; we were not to invade their privacy. I have often wondered why my parents told us this, because I think it would probably have given her pleasure and an interest if we had been allowed to go in and talk to her sometimes.

My father taught us to ride on the basis of this little verse:

Your head and heart keep boldly up,
Your hands and your heels down,
Your knees keep close to your pony's side,
An your elbows close to your own.

We were told that no one could ride until they had fallen off at least fifty times. When I grew out of Nyeupe, I was given a small Somali pony called Panya (or Rat). He had also been brought down from the North by Berkeley Cole. Panya was rather a naughty little pony and had me off most days. I didn't really mind this as I never hurt myself and learnt to fall and keep hold of the reins so as not to let the pony loose. But I think my father thought he was too much for me, so he bought me a lovely mare called Paulette. She was by an Anglo-Arab out of a Somali, and a perfect child's pony. I won a number of show prizes on her and later she bred some very good foals. When we were out with Mohammed Khan and the syces, he used to give us cavalry drill. We had to make a circle with him in the centre giving the orders: 'Walk march! – Tr-r-rot – Right wheel –

Ha-a-alt – Make-much-of-your horses!' and so on which we thought was splendid.

In 1924 some new neighbours arrived to farm the land on the other side of us to the Sladens. They were Major Arthur Dudgeon and his wife Marjorie. Major Dudgeon had come to Kenya almost by chance. He had been born and brought up in Edinburgh at Gogar Bank House (now the residence of the Commander-in-Chief, Scottish Command). After Winchester, he went to Cambridge where he achieved a Double First in science and a half Blue for golf. He was offered a job by Marconi, at that time unknown, but he was not allowed to accept by his father, and instead went to work for the Guinness Brewery in Dublin. He found it dull and resigned, much to the fury of the managing director. He then joined his elder brother gold-mining in Rhodesia, but didn't like that either, came back to Britain, married and decided to emigrate to Canada. They took tickets and sent their heavy luggage to the docks. While Major Dudgeon was standing in a queue waiting to collect the tickets he started to talk to the man behind him, who held forth about British East Africa – 'an earthly paradise, with a perfect climate, good fertile land, almost empty of inhabitants, beautiful scenery and delightful people'. The man in front was told there were no more berths to be had to Canada, so Major Dudgeon, on the spur of the moment, handed him his Canadian tickets and decided to go to Kenya instead. He and his wife retrieved their luggage from the ship and sailed to Africa in October 1913. He brought a Dodge car, which had been the eighth car to be registered in Ireland, and amongst other jobs that he did in Nairobi was to drive this car as a taxi. He would tell his passengers if he took them out to dinner that he wouldn't wait a minute after 10 p.m. He bought some land but it was completely undeveloped and he hadn't the capital to farm it so after the war he took a job in a gold-mine in order to get some money together. This was at a place where the Masai had never seen another white woman. They were very intrigued by Mrs Dudgeon's hair; they wanted to pull it to see if it was real.

The Dudgeon children had been left in Britain with their grandparents and never saw their parents for six years. However, by 1924 the Dudgeons felt able to settle on their land so they brought the children out and started farming. They had three daughters, born within thirteen months; the eldest was Emily and then there were twins, Elizabeth, always called Bissie, and Jean, and then a much younger son, John. The three girls were just a year or two older than us, so they joined in with us and the Sladen girls. Their house was very near the Molo river and not far from where the Rongai station had been built and so we used to go down there on our bicycles. There was only one shop in those days and that was run by two brothers called David and Aaron Reuben. They were Jews who had originally come from Russia and they did not speak English very well. They used to speak to each other in some language which I suppose must have been Yiddish or Russian. They would measure cloth and say: 'A Jew's nose and a robber's arm makes a yard.' We would save up our pocket money, a few shillings, and buy packets of King Stork cigarettes. We always liked the Reuben brothers because they didn't tell our parents what we got up to. We took these cigarettes to the bridge over the Molo river and we used to hide under the bridge and smoke them. We were seven girls together and we would pass the cigarette round and round. Once or twice the Dudgeon girls managed to pinch one of their father's cigars and then we would all have a puff of that.

There was another shop further away which belonged to a man called Taylor. We didn't often go there because it was rather far. Mr Taylor's claim to fame was cutting out people's uvulas. The Africans had a theory that your uvula goes on growing and growing down your throat until you choke and so it was advisable to have it cut out early. So Mr Taylor did a roaring trade with a pair of scissors and some iodine. I think the payment was two shillings or an obligation to purchase goods in his shop. Afterwards the patients would walk round with a handkerchief tied over their mouths until the wound had healed, to prevent the dust getting in. We always knew if someone had had their uvula cut.

My parents did not set much store by formal education. My mother had never been to school; she only had French and German governesses. She had quite a good command of these languages and she was well read. My father, of course, had gone to prep school and then to Eton but he had never taken an exam. It wasn't necessary in those days. He had gone to Oxford to take a degree but he left to fight in the Boer War before he finished his course. So from the time I was about eight and Moy about six we had a series of governesses in Kenya. We had no proper schoolroom; sometimes we did lessons on the verandah, sometimes under a tree in the garden. Moy was apt to cry during lessons and often she had streaming eyes and nose. The governess would tell her 'Go and pick a leaf', and she would use it to mop up her tears. Something always prevented these governesses from staying very long; either they got engaged or they were lonely and wanted to go back to England. I suppose my parents became rather tired of this and decided when I was about ten to send us to Limuru Girls' School, which at that time only had about seventeen children.

We were aged from about six to twelve years. There were two wooden buildings, one the dormitory and the other the classrooms and dining-room. We only had two classes, the 'big ones' and the 'little ones'. We had lessons in two rooms and at the other end was the dining-room. We had outside longdrops – lavatories – as there were no 'pull-and-let-goes', although we did have running water for baths. We led a fairly frugal life; except on Sundays we were not allowed to put butter and jam on our bread, only one or the other. We had maize meal porridge for breakfast, usually burnt and lumpy, with unrefined sugar and milk gone sour, which we hated; for supper we had sweet potato or maize cob. For lunch we had meat and vegetables. We went for walks or ran about all over the place at Limuru; they did try to teach us netball and other games but there were not enough children to make proper teams. We had a system amongst ourselves of slavery, which meant that the head girl was the chief slave master and all the rest of us either slaves or slave owners. Some were both; and during break on Fridays we all had to lie down in the dormitory while the chief slave master beat us with her hair brush. This did not mean that we had done anything bad; it was just general discipline. We were rather cruel; if there was some poor girl we didn't like, we would lock the outside longdrops and post a guard to prevent her entering which meant she had to use the nearest maize field instead. We used to collect safari ants and put them in the piano when the music mistress was trying to play; they would come out and bite her just when she was in the middle of her best piece. One way and another, we were distinctly wild. I supose we were all children of Kenyan pioneers and used to living in wild places.

Once at half-term, which in those days was only a day's outing, we had been sent to Nairobi to spend the day with my parents and in the evening we were sent back to school again with the African driver. And there was the most wonderful sight – the kind of thing every schoolgirl prayed for without much hope. The school had burnt down! It was just a pile of burnt wood and ashes. As it was a holiday, the kitchen *toto*, who was supposed to stoke the fire at intervals all day to heat the bath water, had put on an enormous quantity of wood, enough to last the whole day, and gone off on his own affairs. The metal had become red hot and was touching the wooden sides of the bathroom which started to burn, and nobody being there, the whole dormitory block caught fire. We were put back in the car and returned to Nairobi to my parents who were staying at Chiromo with Sir Northrup and Lady McMillan and I can still remember the horrified look on their faces when we reappeared. We were all sent home for a few weeks until the school managed to find another building, which was Clarence Buxton's house at Tigoni, and we started school again there. There we used to get out of the window at night sometimes and go into the African *shambas* (gardens) that were all round, where we used to dig up and eat their carrots and potatoes. It appears they never complained about this; I suppose we didn't eat very much really.

On Saturdays we were allowed to get out of our gym tunics, shoes and socks which we had to wear on weekdays and get into our khaki shorts with bare feet that we liked best. We used to have picnics by the little streams near the school and one of our favourite pastimes was to go up to the Tigoni police station and watch the *askaris* (soldiers) practising bayoneting. They had stuffed sacks with faces painted on them which they used to rush at and dig their bayonets into.

I never liked school; I found it very tedious and boring and I suppose I was rather spoilt anyhow. After a year or so at the school my parents decided to bring me back to Deloraine and I shared a governess with the Sladen girls. We used to do lessons in a little wooden hut just outside the Sladens' house. Then we had a lovely time riding our ponies and doing what we liked in the evenings.

At Christmas we usually held a party for about a hundred children. We would cut down an acacia thorn tree from the plains and bring it in for a Christmas tree, erect it in the dining-room and ask all the European children from round about.

We had been lent a cottage, what we called a *banda*, at the coast at Likoni, which is on the mainland just near Kilindini Harbour. We went down there for holidays and loved it. It was a small house, thatched with *makuti* (palm leaves) and more or less open air. We used to sleep in half-open rooms and we learnt to swim in the sea which was just below the house. We could watch the ships coming in and out of the harbour. For our shopping we had to take a ferry across the harbour onto the island of Mombasa to a place called Mbaraki and from there walk to where the shops were. In those days the roads were not tarred but were made with white coral which was very glary and hot when walking along the mile or so to town. There was no motor road from Nairobi to Mombasa then so we had come by train and had no car. We had to carry everything. Our chief joy was going to a shop which sold ice creams which were a great treat in the days when fridges were unheard of.

As children we were always left behind when my parents went on their safaris and it wasn't until I was ten years old that I went on my first camping safari. My parents, myself and Moy set off for Tanganyika with

Cocky Blixen. She had married Bror Blixen after he had parted from Karen. The Blixens had a farm at Babati, in Northern Tanganyika and we went down to stay with them. It was tremendous fun and very exciting to be camping in the bush. It took us about three days to reach Babati, where we met Blix. I remember going out shooting kongoni with him. They showed us a silver teapot they had which had been chewed by a hyena who had taken it from their pantry.

3
Settlers and Their Fears

In 1922 the settlers were very worried about what they called the 'Indian Question'. The British Government was proposing to put the Indians on a common franchise with the Europeans, which would mean that the Europeans would eventually be greatly outnumbered once enough Indians had acquired the necessary educational qualifications. There had always been Indians in East Africa trading on the coast, and, as I have said, more came with the railway. There were many more Indians in East Africa than Europeans and the latter felt that if they were put on a common roll with the Indians they would be outvoted and the country would be run as an Indian colony rather than a British colony. They were worried and alarmed about this. They had been encouraged by the British Government to come to a British colony and they had all put money into the country. Many of the settlers had been in India and had seen the poverty and corruption there; they didn't want that to happen in Kenya. Meetings were held about this all over the country. My mother writes of a meeting of settlers over the Indian Question:

On Saturday we went into Nakuru to the big meeting which had been called there to decide on the steps to be taken against the concessions to Indians which is the burning question now . . . the situation is very critical and feeling is running very high. We arrived at the meeting at 2 p.m., Lord Delamere could not be there . . . so Francis was made to take the chair. I was so sorry that he should have no warning on such an important matter. He had never seen the agenda. However, he did it quite well. There was one rather difficult moment when it was suggested that all the white people should refuse to take the oath under the defence force (act) but Francis was able to prevent them putting the resolution before the meeting which I was very glad of, as one hopes very earnestly, that some satisfactory way out of this difficulty may be found without taking so serious a step. After two or three people had spoken more-or-less well, the delegates were chosen to represent the Nakuru District, at the Convention in Nairobi. Four were selected, Francis, Mr Dawson, Mr McLeod and Mr Watkins.

This meeting was held in August 1922, after which there was much negotiating with the British Government. On 31 January 1923 my mother describes another meeting:

Francis and I went to a mass meeting of settlers on the Indian Question in Nakuru. A despatch has been received that gives the Indians all their demands. The franchise, no restriction of immigration, no segregation, etc. It is almost unbelievable. The meeting was interesting as the whole thing had been arranged in two days and it was amazing to see the number of people. I was very impressed by their appearance, mostly men between thirty and forty with good strong, courageous faces, clean and virile, fine material. We had an excellent man named Thackrah in the chair independent of all parties. Francis and Lord Delamere sat on either side. Lord Delamere was in a terribly difficult position as he is on the Executive Council at which everything is supposed to be secret but he made the most admirable speech though he was plainly weighing every word he spoke. Francis also made two good speeches begging everyone to be cautious and to take no isolated action. A resolution was eventually unanimously carried that, every constitutional means to avoid being swamped by Indians in the Government of this Colony were to be tried but if these failed we should be compelled to become rebels. It is a dreadful situation! In my heart I don't feel the Home Government will force it and have another civil war on their hands. The Indians in this country with the exception of Shastri, who was a paid agitator, would be easy to satisfy. None of the sensible people out here want to prevent the Indians having representation but they do want to be assured that the whites will not be swamped by the Indians in the Government, or that the whole country will not be flooded by Indians and made impossible as a white colony. There were several very good speeches and out of that body of several hundred men only one man who withdrew rather than agree to the resolution. They then voted for their group commander; Francis was unamimously chosen which means he has to organize this enormous district . . . I am glad to say he has most efficient district leaders under him including General Sladen.

As early as 1921 my father had taken Lord Delamere's place temporarily as member for the Rift Valley in the Legislative Council while he was away. My father had only just completed his two years in the country as a necessary qualification. My mother says that she thought Lord Delamere a great darling, most amusing and such a gentleman with beautiful manners, but she doesn't think he should be treated with quite such deference. She says: 'The Governor isn't in it anywhere.' The Governor, Sir Edward Grigg (later Lord Altrincham) had arrived in the colony only in 1925, and at first found it hard to cope with the rumbustious personality of Lord Delamere (who stayed with us sometimes, but I can't remember him, only that my mother told me that he did not like sheets on his bed, only blankets, and he had to have a lighted hurricane lamp in his room all night).

In 1924 my father was elected as a delegate to go to Tanganyika to a conference to be held at Tukuyu on Closer Union. There were delegates coming from Uganda, Tanganyika, Nyasaland, Rhodesia, North and

South, and Kenya. This conference had been organized by Lord Delamere as he wanted to get all the white settlers from all these countries together to discuss how they could form one big white dominion from Rhodesia to the Sudan. Lord Delamere organized the conference entirely at his own expense. He took down all his own plates and silver and arranged the accommodation for everybody. The delegates, including my parents, all drove down to Southern Tanganyika by car and back again – a thousand miles each way on very bad roads. My mother describes the conference as follows:

> Lord D was in the chair, which in a way ties his hands unfortunately, but he is so courteous and tactful with everyone and manages them all beautifully. They discussed many subjects, almost the most interesting of them was the linking up by railway the whole of Africa from Egypt to the Cape. What a wonderful thing this is, even surpassing Rhodes's dreams, and when one looks at little Lord D in his old brown sweater with his colossal head and long hair, pointing with his stick to the map on the wall and listens to him explaining his ideas so humbly, one realizes what great achievements this one private individual has been able to accomplish, and one is very proud to be associated with him in however humble a way . . .

Closer Union never came about – there was too much opposition from the Colonial Government, on the ground that the Africans didn't want to be dominated by the Europeans.

In 1925, when Sir Northrup McMillan died, my father was asked to take his place in the Legislative Council for the Ukambani constituency. He was also approached to stand for the Nyeri constituency in the place of Berkeley Cole, but he decided that he was committed to Ukambani. When my mother first saw his constituents she thought them 'a queer rough-looking lot of men sitting on packing cases . . .' She goes on:

> I was terrified, and Francis's voice sounded nervous to me the first few sentences, after that he warmed up and was really quite excellent. I was surprised as he had not prepared a regular speech, he just outlined what his policy would be on the big imperial questions, hardly glanced at his headings. He really spoke admirably and sincerely. He was very well received. I was amazed as he was a total stranger in this district. I said to one man after the meeting that I thought it so nice of them to trust a man they didn't know and he replied: 'But he knows the world, Lady Francis, and we know that we can trust him and that is why we want him to represent us.'

They said he knew the world and it was true that my father was very closely connected with some of the politicians in England, particularly those in the Conservative Party. The Duke of Devonshire, who disturbed many settlers when he said as Secretary of State for the Colonies that African interests should be paramount, was married to his first cousin, Evelyn. Earl Winterton, then Under-Secretary of State for India, was also his first cousin. Lord Lansdowne, who was the Foreign Secretary who had arranged the Entente Cordiale with France, was his uncle by marriage and he was on intimate terms with many of the men in the Government of that time. He used to correspond with many of these people and many years later I found a letter amongst his correspondence from Neville Chamberlain, then Chancellor of the Exchequer, saying: 'My dear Francis, please stop writing me such stinkers. It makes one disinclined to reply.' I don't know if he always wrote 'stinkers' but he certainly pulled no punches in his arguments with people in England about Kenya.

In 1926 my parents went to Livingstone (near Victoria Falls) for the second Closer Union Conference. They went by ship and they were asked to meet Sir Donald Cameron, the Governor of Tanganyika, while on the way. When they reached Dar-es-Salaam my mother writes:

We hoped to reach Dar-es-Salaam, the 'Haven of Peace', tonight in time for Francis to see Sir Donald Cameron. He is considered a very able but very truculent man, and he is evidently very suspicious of Grigg (Governor of Kenya) wishing to run him, which is not the case. Only Grigg sees the big vision of Africa and Cameron concentrates on every detail and dots every 'i' and crosses every 't'. We reached Dar-es-Salaam before four o'clock, much sooner than we expected. A very rough sea and we anchored four miles out. Sir Donald sent his private secretary to invite us to dinner. My heart sank! However, they assured me that the wind always dropped at seven o'clock and sure enough it did. A huge launch was sent for us but she still plunged a bit and we got pretty covered in spray. I luckily was in a mackintosh over my evening gown. It was a full moon and when we got into the harbour we were taken up a little still lagoon overhung by palm trees, tall and black against the sky. The sand almost as white as snow in the moonlight, nothing could have exceeded it in beauty. We then drove in a most luxurious car to Government House, a huge Eastern house all black and white tiles, white walls and black pillars, enormous verandahs and open balconies, not beautiful but quite effective and good for entertaining. Lady Cameron is a nice woman, peaceful and restful but looked as though she had spent too long in the East. I sat next to Sir Donald, a very curious man, he was charming to me. He is so much more Oriental than Western. He was born in the West Indies and I wonder what his parentage is? He said he longed to retire to Japan and become a Buddhist priest and then, of course, I realized he was exactly like one. I could see his yellow face and slanting eyes, enigmatical smile, sitting on the floor in a rather dirty kimono in contemplation. We had an excellent dinner. The interior is deep pink which causes the moonlit sky seen through the arches to appear green. It was exactly like a scene on the stage. After dinner we left Francis and Sir Donald to have their talk and we motored along the sea for about seven miles to a renowned place called Oyster Bay, very beautiful, but I was very tired and beginning to long for my bed.

In 1931 my father was chosen to represent the Kenya settlers at the Joint Parliamentary Commission in London. After Lord Delamere's death, he was elected unopposed as member for the Rift Valley, Lord Delamere's old constituency, and became Leader of the Elected Members in Lord Delamere's stead as well as a member of the Executive Council. His two rivals for the position were Major Ewart Grogan and Major Ferdinand Cavendish-Bentinck and I think they were both rather disappointed that my father was put at the head. When my mother went to Uganda in 1925 she had met Major Cavendish-Bentinck, who was private secretary to the Governor and she wrote:

After dinner I talked to Major Cavendish-Bentinck, a curious creature. He is silent almost to the verge of rudeness but somehow he is rather nice and I like him and in the end he has talked to me a great deal. He, I gather, is unhappily married and I think his point of view about everything is a little distorted and warped.

Later, Cavendish-Bentinck came to live in Kenya and eventually became a minister and also the Speaker in the Legislative Council. Shortly before he died he succeeded a cousin as 8th Duke of Portland.

In his book *Africa, Kenya's Opportunity*, Lord Altrincham, who, as Sir Edward Grigg, had been the Governor of Kenya from 1925 to 1930, describes Lord Delamere and my father as follows:

Lord Delamere was a great man in his own world and would have been an even greater one with influence, like Rhodes, in England as well as Africa but for certain accidents of upbringing and weaknesses which narrowed his vivid intelligence. I might be Governor of the Colony, but when I arrived in 1925 he was the uncrowned King. The first real settler, to whom all subsequent ones looked up to for leadership and initiated blood brother of the Masai; profoundly respected by them for the scope and variety of his pastoral activities, a generous dispenser of hospitality whose parties at the Muthaiga Club were already legendary and to crown all, a temperament so rollicking and friendly, though so fiery that he might have been sixteen when he was sixty. Towards me, he conducted himself with a courtesy and deference which had the easy dignity of the eighteenth century. I do not remember a single occasion on which he lost this grace, in private or public. There I was, many years his junior and a sore trial to his usually short-lived patience. Very early therefore, in our association I conceived an admiration and affection for him which I have reason to know that he returned, though relations were often strained between us by political disagreement. His power declined about the middle of my term and for a short time he resigned the leadership of the Elected Members to Lord Francis Scott. But whether leader or not he was always a great man of the Colony to whom it owed, and will always owe, the success and high quality of its settlement. There were two ways however, in which he was most unlike Rhodes, and both told heavily against his achievement. First of these, was his upbringing. He had succeeded to a title and great possessions when very young, and had always got what he wanted without much effort until he turned in his late twenties from recreation to creative work. Rhodes made his way by sheer greatness of mind and character. He had no other advantage. Delamere, moreover, was completely devoid of financial instinct. He had been accustomed from very early youth to easy affluence and his indifference to the money aspect of any project, a dinner, a dam, or design or any order was proverbial; he would spend without thought and lived by the goodwill of banks on uncertain security for years after he had spent his private fortune. But all this financial profligacy, let us never forget, was devoted to the progress and welfare of the Colony which can never overestimate what it owes to him . . .

Delamere's Deputy Leader was Lord Francis Scott who had none of Delamere's popular gifts. His great handicap was the loss of a leg due to a war wound which caused him constant pain and made him fiercely impatient at public meetings and other fixtures unnecessarily prolonged. The latter part of his life was overshadowed by that trial but he always held the trust of his constituency in my time. He was a most faithful disciple of his Chief, but as utterly unlike him as a human being could be, a disciplined Grenadier by training, with a reserved and aristocratic cast of mind. He had none of Delamere's gay decorum and never embarked on any enterprise, public or private, without counting the cost of it. In politics, as in polo, he rode as straight as a die and invariably spoke his mind. But he had little care for political or constitutional issues beyond the obvious questions of the day. As leader he extracted complete loyalty from the other Elected Members . . . In debate, Scott spoke clearly and to the point, never wasting words. I found him much easier to do business with than Delamere, both in Executive Council land in private conference. Not that he had any more idea than Delamere of appeasing a Governor. He was Delamere's alter-ego on all questions of policy, great and small, never departed by an inch from the line he had decided to take but he is less stormy than Delamere and much quicker to realize and accept the fact when his line was definitely blocked. I had a deep respect and affection for him, his public spirit was noble and none of the early settlers I knew, excepting Delamere, rendered Kenya a better service.

In fact, Lord Altrincham was not correct when he said that my father suffered constant pain in his leg. Having been shot through his sciatic nerve he had no feeling in his leg at all. Later he had arthritis in his hip which did cause him pain and he had his wounded leg amputated in 1933. I'm afraid my father's impatience and short temper was merely because he did not suffer fools gladly and he was sometimes very impatient with the slow-thinking, narrow-mindedness of some of his colleagues.

4
Visiting Britain

Until I was eighteen we used to travel to England by boat every two and a half years or so and spend about six months there. At that time it was not thought good for Europeans, either mentally or physically, to stay too long at a high altitude under the equatorial sun. All Government officials were forced to take what was known as 'home leave'. They couldn't spend their leave in Kenya even if they wanted to, but were obliged to go to Europe. It was supposed to freshen their minds and broaden their views. So we too used to shut up the house, leave the farm in charge of a manager and take a boat to England.

As children we had great fun aboard the boat, dashing all round the decks and up and down the gangways. The sailors were always very kind to us but I am sure we must have been very tiresome, making all that noise and disturbing other passengers, especially when it was rough at sea and people were lying in the deck chairs feeling seasick. We would rush round and round to see how far we could get before another wave knocked us over, sometimes on top of the poor people in the deck chairs. We would also climb up and stick our heads through the toilet portholes and 'boo' the occupants, much to their consternation. But we did at the same time have an opportunity of seeing many different places and people. We stopped at Aden where we would be taken ashore to see the 'mummies' – these were really dugongs which are supposed to be mermaids but they looked more like long brown cigars about the size of a woman. Then we went to Port Sudan where we saw the sand dunes and camels and went out in glass-bottomed boats to watch fish swimming about in the coral. Port Said was always enjoyable because of the 'gully-gully' men. They came on board with live day-old chicks and they said 'Gully-gully-gully' all the time. They told fortunes and did conjuring tricks, turning money or rings or watches into chicks and back again, or pulling chicks out of people's noses. They would borrow people's rings and toss them into the sea and bring them back again. They also addressed people by the names of celebrities: my mother would be called Mrs Pankhurst and my father Lloyd George, both people they strongly disliked. We loved watching them. We also went ashore where there was a large shop called Simon Artz where we bought all kinds of odds and ends.

Once through the Suez Canal and into the Mediterranean we would pass Cyprus and Crete, sometimes with snow on the mountains. We saw smoke coming out of Stromboli and thought the little village nestling at its foot looked in a very dangerous position. Once the boat developed engine trouble and we only got as far as Messina in Sicily, where they announced that the boat could go no further and all the passengers would have to do the rest of the journey by train. We spent a lovely few days at Taormina and then went by train to London, travelling up the length of Italy, through Switzerland, to Paris and then to London. I was about fourteen and it was the first time I had seen Europe apart from Britain, and I enjoyed every moment. In Sicily, Loder was sent to see the luggage on to the train and had been given some Italian money to pay the porters. When my father asked for some of it back, he found she had changed it all into English. She thought that once you were on the railway you were more or less on English soil and had no more need of foreign exchange. He had to change it back and lost on the exchange both ways.

We had no home of our own in England so we used to stay with various relations, moving about from one to the other. We always had some kind of attendant, a nanny or governess, and we were parked in different places in their care whilst my parents went off and did what they had to do. When in London, we usually stayed at 18 Carlton House Terrace, my uncle John Astor's house. It was a large house at the very end of Carlton House Terrace, just opposite the Admiralty and Horse Guards Parade, and a marvellous place for watching any processions there might be. You entered through a marble hall lined with Canalettos and there was a large table which had every kind of article left on it for collection, from plants and saddles to couturier dresses and boxes of jewels. A huge staircase with a red carpet led up to a gallery all round the top. Occasionally, when my Aunt Vi gave a ball, we were allowed to hide behind the pillars in the gallery and watch the people as they went in to dinner wearing their jewels, orders and diamond tiaras. The footmen, for these special occasions, were still dressed in knee-breeches with powdered hair. Then there was a big dining-room with a massive long table. Sometimes at a family gathering of all the cousins of several generations, we might be over thirty people round the table. Upstairs there was a ballroom and my aunt's sitting-room and a room we called the mirror room; all four walls and even the ceiling were entirely covered in mirror. As you walked in you saw innumerable images of yourself; as children we loved watching ourselves doing different antics. On the next floor up were the nurseries, the schoolroom and the bedrooms. It was a rule of the house that unless specially invited into the dining-room, we always took our meals in the nurseries regardless of age. Later, when I was grown up, I can remember breakfast was always an interesting meal as you never knew who was staying in the house; people would come and go and we breakfasted in our dressing gowns. It was very informal and great fun.

Then we went on to stay at Hever Castle near Edenbridge in Kent which was Aunt Vi's and Uncle John's country home. This was an amazing place. It had been bought by Uncle John's father, the first Lord Astor, who was entirely American but became very attached to Britain. He eventually came over to live here, became a naturalized Englishman and Viscount Astor. He also bought Cliveden, where eventually his eldest son Waldorf lived. His younger son, John, who married Aunt Vi, was given Hever. He was Member of Parliament for Dover for many years.

Hever dated originally from the thirteenth century; it had belonged to the Boleyns and Henry VIII had courted Anne there. When Lord Astor bought it, it was very tumbledown and more or less used for cattle barns. He was inspired to repair it and restore it to its original splendour, with a moat all round. He even built a Tudor village round it. It was always known as the village, but it was really a series of Tudor-like cottages which were joined together with passages and made into suites where his guests could stay. Outwardly it did look very like a village – except, of course, that it had no roads or shops – and it was surrounded by beautiful gardens. Lord Astor made an Italian garden which he filled with marble statues and by damming the river he created a large ornamental lake. At the end of the garden was a piazza of marble. Hever was a wonderful place to stay in as children. We had ponies, a lake and river to boat on and swim in, caves to explore, a golf course, a tennis court and a maze. But above all Aunt Vi and Uncle John made it such a happy home, not only for their own children but for us and our other cousins, all of whom used to stay there for long periods.

Aunt Vi, who worked hard for various charities, was by nature a very frugal person; she hated waste or unnecessary expense. Her great sef-indulgence, if you could call it that, was her horses; she kept some hunters in Leicestershire and would go there to hunt whenever she could. She rode beautifully, always side-saddle. She also loved her garden and spent much time working out plans with the head gardener.

There were some little brown dogs at Hever which Uncle John called 'golden terriers'. They were all descended from a mongrel dog and bitch that he had got in France during the First World War and had become very very inbred. Uncle John adored them and they could do no wrong; he used to have up to five of them sleeping on his bed at night. They were very spoiled and lay on all the chairs, so that at times the humans had to sit on the floor. They were also very nervy and used to snap and bite at the slightest provocation.

Aunt Vi had five children. Margaret and George were by her first husband, Charlie Fitzmaurice – George later became Lord Lansdowne because his father's eldest brother's three sons all died; the eldest fell under an underground train and the second and third were killed in the war within a week of each other. There were three Astor boys, Gavin, Hugh and John. In age I come between George and Gavin, and Moy between Gavin and Hugh.

Uncle John had an organ in the hall on which he enjoyed playing in the evenings when there was no party staying. His other relaxation was painting in oils. Winston Churchill lived not very far away at Chartwell and he used to come over sometimes and join Uncle John when he was sketching in the garden. I can remember him arriving with a procession of retainers carrying his easel, paint box, brushes, etc. One day when I was about twelve he caught sight of me and said, 'You come from Kenya, don't you?' I answered 'Yes' and he commented 'Horrible country.' His second daughter, Sarah, was a little older than I and when I was sent to school in Paris my aunt arranged for me to travel with her. When I 'came out' in London the Churchills once asked me to dinner, and I made a fool of myself by sitting on an antique chair that was not meant for sitting on, and it collapsed under me. I shall always remember the beauty and dignity of Clemmie Churchill. She used to be outstanding amongst the other chaperones at the balls I went to.

Uncle John Astor had bought *The Times* in 1923 and there were often a number of *Times* people staying, frequently including the Editor. Every summer there was a '*Times* Day' at Hever and the house and garden were open to all the *Times* employees. They would come in buses in a huge party and go swimming or boating and wander round the gardens where there was a band playing and food laid on for them. It was always a very happy day.

Uncle John's other big interest was the Middlesex Hospital and he was Chairman of the Board of Governors. He had been wounded in the war and lost a leg and he felt he owed a debt to the doctors who had saved his life. He paid for the building of the nurses' home and later when he had to go and live in the South of France he had two cottages in the grounds, one of which he used to lend to the medical students and the other to the nurses. They used to come out in relay parties and stay in these cottages for their holidays, all paid for by Uncle John. He was a generous and thoughtful man.

In the Twenties and Thirties, these large houses were still run in quite grand style, with a housekeeper and numerous housemaids. There was a French chef with four or five kitchen maids and there was a butler and a groom of the chambers and several footmen, as well as grooms and gardeners outside. The ladies who came to stay had their maids and the men their valets. A charming custom was that every evening the gardeners would find out from the maids what colour dress their ladies would be wearing and there would be a suitable posy on their dressing table that they could wear for dinner.

My uncle and aunt used to give weekend parties and all kinds of people were invited – politicians, maybe the Prime Minister, ambassadors, writers, painters; so from nursery days on the family would mix with all these distinguished guests. If you were still in the nursery, under the age of eight, you had all your meals with the nannies but after this age you were expected to lunch in the dining-room. We used to have to run down to lunch punctually, all clean and tidy, and say 'How do you do' to everyone. We had to learn how to be polite at meals and how to talk to our neighbours and generally behave properly. Sometimes we were allowed to go down for tea also, but supper and breakfast were always in the nursery or schoolroom with nanny or the governess. The long passages were wonderful for running down; one was reputed to be a quarter of a mile long. There were also underground passages which were paved in stone and these were very good for roller-skating.

We also used to stay with my grandmother, Mary Minto, at Hydon End, near Godalming. She had bought the house when she had to leave Minto when her son, Larry, was married. She made a lovely garden there. We were given a room for a nursery or a schoolroom and used to stay for several weeks at a time. There were bluebells in the woods and we would climb Hydon Hill and eat the wild bilberries that grew there. Although she could be quite strict, my grandmother had a wonderful sense of humour and we adored her. She was lady-in-waiting to Queen Mary and when I was eight and staying with her in London, Queen Mary gave a children's tea party at Marlborough House, although she lived in those days at Buckingham Palace. She had no grandchildren yet but her own children were all grown up, so she asked my grandmother if she would provide a suitable child. As it was my birthday, my grandmother thought of me. So off we set to Buckingham Palace, me dressed in my best. We arrived there and sat in a small round room to wait for Queen Mary to come down. My grandmother had instructed me that I must curtsy and kiss her hand when she arrived. I managed this all right and then we went out and drove off in one of those big Daimlers that the Royal Family used, the Queen and my grandmother sitting together at the back and I on one of the little tip-down seats in front of them. I'm told that I asked Queen Mary whether, as she was a queen, she had diamonds on her sponge. Queen Mary laughed and said she didn't and was rather glad; she thought they would be very scratchy. We drove down the Mall to Marlborough House and went and sat on some little gold chairs out in the garden and of course, as we were with the Queen, we sat in the front row. I sat between the Queen and my grandmother. Then a terrifying creature appeared. It was a short fat little creature like a man but its face was completely white with a huge red mouth and funny eyes and a funny hat. Coming from Africa, I had never seen or heard of a clown and I thought it must be a spirit or a witch doctor. To my horror it came towards us, getting closer and closer. So I'm sorry to say that I got up from my chair and deserted my post and ran. I disappeared into the crowd. After a bit of frantic searching I luckily found my mother and was told that I had behaved very badly. However, Queen Mary didn't seem to take offence, because later when I was ill she sent me a present and a very nice card. She wrote on the card, 'To dear little Pamela with best love, from the Queen, and hoping she will soon be well again.' She also later on sent me another present for my birthday and on this card she wrote 'For Pamela Scott, with love and best wishes, from the Queen.' I have still got these cards and the presents.

We also stayed with Uncle John and Aunt Margaret Buccleuch in Scotland. Aunt Margaret must have been very pretty as a girl but when I remember her she was a very quiet and rather mousey old lady, the mother of eight children. She had a very simple mind and there were a great many stories told in the family about her naiveté. Once the famous actor Beerbohm Tree came to see her. When the butler announced 'Mr Tree to see your Grace', she supposed it must be one of the foresters. Another time one of her sisters-in-law, having heard that she had been unwell, went to see her and said she hoped that she was better and that it had been nothing serious. Aunt Margaret thanked her, said she was quite recovered and thought it wasn't anything much – 'only this VD that everyone seems to be getting these days'. She had a mania for economy and it was said that when she died she was still wearing the underclothes that she had had in her bridal trousseau. She was supposed to have died of malnutrition and to have had £25,000 in her current account at the time.

We sometimes stayed at Drumlanrig Castle in Dumfriesshire. It is a most beautiful place, built in pinkish stone, and lies in a valley by the River Nith with heather-covered hills round it. Once a visitor's servant asked 'Why has your master no park wall?' and was told: 'These hills are the park walls.' My father used to go grouse shooting on the hills. We were allowed as children to go with the ladies. The men would go fairly early in the morning to be followed by the ladies later with the luncheon. We were allowed to sit in the butts with the guns if we kept quiet and squatted down out of the way, and then we used to help retrieve the birds at the end of the drive. There would be a wonderful picnic lunch, with cold grouse and salmon and after lunch a few more drives. Sometimes we would be allowed to ride the shooting ponies back to the castle, and it always amused us that when we passed through the villages, the ponies would automatically turn into the pubs and stand there as though they were expecting to wait a while. It rather gave away the stable boys.

Drumlanrig Castle was full of art treasures, pictures, tapestries and furniture, none of which we appreciated as children, but it was rather fun sleeping in the big four-poster beds though rather creepy at night walking down the passages and up the winding staircases. There were four turrets with winding staircases; each was marked with a different colour and you followed the lines and arrows along the walls showing you which way to go. There was a blue turret, a green one and a red, and you had to remember which colour to follow to get to your bedroom. As small children we often slept in the nurseries which were at the top of one of these turrets. Moy and I used to get very frightened up in these rooms; we used to climb into bed together and hug each other. It wasn't till years later that I discovered this nursery was supposed to be haunted. It had been made into a nursery because people thought that children would not hear that it was haunted and therefore would not be frightened – but we were!

Loder usually came with us. On her first visit she was trying to make the fire burn in my mother's bedroom and it wouldn't draw. She looked out of the window and saw a man outside in a green baize apron and a bowler hat and with an ''Ere you', summoned him to give a hand. The housekeeper at the time had once been a cook and according to Loder's rigid ideas it was quite wrong to promote a cook to a housekeeper. The failure of the fire seemed a natural consequence. Anyway, the man came up, bent down on his knees and fixed the fire. Telling the story that evening, she ended: 'And oo, m'lady, all the time, it was 'is Grace!' He often walked about in a green baize apron because he was frequently hanging pictures. The Buccleuchs had so many pictures that there wasn't room for them all on walls at once, so they had to store some away and were frequently changing them round. My uncle liked this job – he was rather an eccentric man. He always wore his bowler hat because he was bald and it kept his head warm.

He had been in the Navy as a young man and would always shout at people, because he had grown used to shouting against the wind when at sea. He had a very loud voice and was apt to greet people when they arrived with: 'Hello, very nice to see you. What train are you leaving on?' This wasn't because he was anxious for them to leave immediately, but because he loved looking up the train times on the timetable. However, people who knew him well would volunteer when they arrived: 'Oh hello John. I'm leaving 10.45 on Tuesday the 15th,' or whatever. His pet hate was Roman Catholics. So if a Roman Catholic came he would say: 'Hello. To hell with the Pope.' Another of his strange habits was that at meal times he would take out his false teeth and swish them about in the finger bowl that came with the fruit and sometimes he would forget them there. After dinner when we were all in the drawing-room, the footman would bring them in on a silver tray and say: 'Your teeth, your Grace.' He was very kind and generous and often would say to us children: 'Got any money?' To which of course we would always reply 'No.' 'Well, here's a quid,' and he would give us a pound note which to us in those days was a fortune.

When the railways were built in Britain in the 1840s the Duke of Buccleuch at the time made an agreement that where a line passed over his land he would have the right to stop a train at any time and get in or out of it. This was still in force in the days when I was a child and it used to be rather exciting when one went to stay in one of the Buccleuch houses. The Scottish express would suddenly come to a grinding halt at a wayside station and give us all time to get out with our luggage; likewise it would stop if we wanted to board. I think my uncle had to telephone the station master some time beforehand to arrange this and I don't think the railway people liked us doing it very much; it must have upset their regular timetables.

Another of the Buccleuch houses where we stayed was Langholm Lodge which was a shooting lodge and comparatively small though most people would consider it quite large. There was excellent grouse shooting there and in 1911 they got the record bag for Scotland of 2,523 grouse on a beat called Roan Fell. Sometimes when we arrived the house was full with guns, wives, loaders, maids, dogs and general entourage and so we children were billeted on the head keeper. Mrs Smith used to prepare wonderful meals for us – particularly the huge teas with delicious cakes and scones – and we always enjoyed staying there.

Sometimes we used to stay with my father's bachelor brother, Henry. He lived in a place called Gledswood, near Melrose. This was a small Georgian house and he had a small property of a hundred acres or so which went right down to the River Tweed. There the Tweed meets the River Leader and there is good fishing. Uncle Henry's household consisted of Mrs Eddie, his cook-housekeeper and Ernest Simpson, his butler-valet. Simpson was a Cockney and used to call Loder 'the Queen of Tanjanyika'. I think he had originally been a footman at Montagu House. He was married to a former kitchen maid of the Buccleuchs, who said she had been sacked because she had sent peas up to the dining-rooom in cream instead of butter. They had a daughter, Gwen, who was about my age and we used to play together. There was also a little boy who helped Simpson whose name was Willie Armstrong. My uncle always called him 'young Gilknockie', after the famous freebooter in the past called Willie Armstrong of Gilknockie. Later he became a policeman in Edinburgh and married Gwen Simpson. Uncle Henry always had a labrador or two and a Border terrier called Sandy. We used to stay there for quite long periods whilst our parents went away on their own. Just above Gledswood is a hill, Bemersyde, at the top of which there is a road to Scott's View, where Sir Walter Scott used to stand looking at the view across the Tweed Valley. From here you can see the three Eildon Hills. The story goes that originally there was only one but Michael Scott, the Wizard, cut it in half one night and the third hill was the mound of earth he had dug out from between them. They are a famous landmark in the Borders.

Often we used to stay at Minto, my mother's old home, which was a lovely house and had beautiful gardens. The house had a special scent, which came from the flowers which always filled the rooms. We enjoyed staying with my Uncle Larry and his Canadian wife, Marion. We would go up to the village and see all the old people who remembered my mother as a child. We climbed the Minto Craigs which are a rocky escarpment and at their top was a place called Barnhill's Bed and Fat Lips Castle. There was once a robber who used to live up there called Fat Lips. He used to watch for the coaches coming by on the Edinburgh to Carlisle Road which passes underneath along the Teviot River. When he saw a likely-looking coach approaching he would rush down and hold them up.

'Your money or your life.' There is also a small grassy hill known as Minto Hill which my mother says she used to slide down on her bottom when she was a girl.

5
School in Europe

When I was about twelve, my parents decided that we ought to be a little bit more Europeanized and they decided to leave us in England for a while. So we went to stay with our Aunt Vi and Uncle John Astor and they engaged a governess called Miss Brewin for us. We used to stay all the week in Carlton House Terrace doing lessons in the schoolroom in the mornings and then in the afternoons we used to be taken out and shown the sights, the Tower of London, Westminster Abbey, the Mint and so on. Sometimes we were taken to a play or a concert. The weekends we spent at Hever Castle. But we always longed to be back in Kenya and after we had been in England for about a year my parents decided to bring us back. We were absolutely delighted and it was arranged that we should travel on a Union Castle boat via Cape Town. Off we set with Miss Brewin. We went to the Canary Islands first and then to St Helena. There we got into a horse-drawn carriage which took us right up steep hills covered in arum lilies to the house in which Napoleon had lived. Next we went to Cape Town, where we took a trip up Table Mountain in a cable car. Then we progressed up the east coast of Africa, stopping at the different ports. At Port Elizabeth there was a snake park; at Durban we went for a bus ride up in the Valley of a Thousand Hills and were taken to see a Zulu family. I remember there was an old man there who never cut his nails; he had huge long nails, about ten inches long, and very horrible they were. At Beira we went in a little boat to look at the sugar factory and at Mozambique we were taken to see the fort. We walked round the top of the fort and looked down into the compounds full of prisoners. We were told all the prisioners in one compound were convicted murderers. Then we went to Zanzibar and eventually we reached Mombasa, and back to Deloraine. We were so happy to get back and there we stayed, being taught by Miss Brewin, until I was fifteen.

My parents then decided that we should be sent to an English girls' boarding school. We were taken back to England and sent to Downe House, near Newbury. To me this was awful; I really hated it. I was almost sixteen and it was very painful for me to be put into a very ugly school uniform and to sleep in a cold dormitory – the window was wide open and we were only allowed a certain number of blankets. The food was horrible too and of course there was the usual discipline and regimentation of school life which I had never experienced before.

I hated the austerity of it, the ugly rooms with no flowers and no comfortable furniture. I'd been brought up in a luxurious house with beautiful things around me – either that or in a mud hut! – and to live in this barrack-like atmosphere really depressed me. Sometimes I would go to the passage that led to the head mistress's quarters where there was a carpet and a table with a bowl of flowers on it. I would go there just to remind myself of something which looked a little more civilized. They used to try and make me play lacrosse but I'd never played any games and I had no aptitude for them in any case. So I really was rather miserable. The only thing I enjoyed at all was that three girls together were allowed to take bicycles and go wherever they liked. There were tree plantations and forest nearby and I loved to go there if I could manage to find two other girls to go with me. This wasn't always easy because I had come when I was much older than the others and everybody had already made their own friends. But I did find people sometimes and we used to cycle into the woods and have picnics and I felt a little more at home. I met a classmate of mine a few years ago and she told me that when I arrived at school I was to them like an exotic butterfly! This quite surprised me but I suppose they found me very strange.

The form that I was in was being taught for the School Certificate; however, as I hadn't done earlier parts of the course, nor had I ever studied chemistry, biology, or anything of that sort, I couldn't take the examination, so my parents thought they might as well take me away again. Moy stayed there a while longer; she settled down better than I, being younger. My parents didn't believe in taking examinations in any case. They said they had never taken any examinations themselves and thought they made people very narrow-minded, because you had to concentrate on certain subjects to the exclusion of all else. They thought it much better to have a broader education and learn more general knowledge. Of course, they didn't realize that to get a job you needed evidence of having passed some examination or other.

Soon after we went to Downe House, we were allowed to come to London for half term. It was the Eton and Harrow Match and we were invited to a teenage dance which was being given by Lord and Lady Astor (Waldorf, my Uncle John's elder brother, and his wife Nancy) at their St James's Square house. They used to give a party every summer for the

Eton and Harrow weekend. We were invited to dine with Lord and Lady Halifax before the dance and my mother was with us. We put on our best dresses, which were short, flowered chiffon. At the Halifax's we found some other girls about our own age who had tremendously smart, long white crinoline dresses, quite unlike ours, and smart coiffures – my hair was scraped back into a ponytail and Moy's was cropped short. Even though I was just sixteen, I had hardly ever had dinner in the dining-room. At home we had always had our supper on a tray and I was bewildered by all the cutlery on the table. I also found it quite difficult to talk to the other guests. After dinner we went on to the Astors' house. There I had a stand-up argument with my mother because she, having observed my unmade-up face – not to mention all the other girls in beautiful long dresses and us in short ones – decided she would like me to powder my nose and put on some lipstick. I flatly refused. I felt I would look an awful fool. I had never done such a thing before and nothing would make me do as I was asked. Having become rather bad-tempered, I went out of the room and seeing a lot of people climbing the stairs, decided to follow. When I reached the top, there was a man in livery who asked me my name. I told him and to my horror I heard him shouting it out across the room. I had done completely the wrong thing. I should have waited for my mother and Lady Halifax and the rest of our party and we would all have gone up together and been announced. I really felt that I had done everything wrong and I didn't enjoy the evening at all. I didn't know anyone to dance with, had never been to a dance and didn't know how to dance. The whole evening was very distressing.

I was taken away from boarding school and sent to a finishing school in Paris. This finishing school was run by a Russian family and most of the girls were American. It was in Auteuil, a suburb of Paris. I really enjoyed this but I was very strange compared to the American girls and they thought it was extraordinary that I knew nothing about make-up and wore long bloomers with elastic round my knees; that I had never had a pair of high-heeled shoes and that I knew nothing about films and film stars and had only rarely been to the cinema. However, I found the American girls much more broad-minded than those in England and easier to get on with. The English girls I found very parochial, having never travelled anywhere. They could only talk about village life, hunt balls and such things. I had no idea what a hunt ball was. They liked tennis parties and I couldn't play the game. I had really very little in common with them, whereas the American girls were from all sorts of places and several of them were children of film stars and had travelled a great deal.

The Russians who ran the school were Prince and Princess Meshchersky. They were refugees and had had to leave Russia during the Revolution. They used to tell us terrifying stories about their escape and how people had been killed. Russians seem to like gruesome details and they could be very morbid sometimes. We were taken on outings to museums and the Louvre and other galleries. At the Louvre there was one room where they had marble statues of dead people lying as if in their graves and starting to decompose with worms coming out of their stomachs. The Russians always seemed to like this room the best; they would tell us: 'You must remember we're Asiatics, we're not Europeans.' (Indeed the Meshchersky princes were of Tatar origin.) They had no sense of time; day and night were the same to them. They were also quite fatalistic and never looked before crossing the street in Paris, saying that they had nothing to live for in any case. A lot of their friends were taxi-drivers and some of the girls were models. Often, when we took a taxi and gave the address, the driver would say, 'Oh yes, how is the Princess? I'm coming to dinner next week.' And it would transpire that the taxi-driver too was a prince. Many of the girls were models in the big houses like Molyneux or Schiaparelli. They were terribly impractical. Sometimes they would spend all their money on a beautiful dress and leave themselves with no money to buy food. They would come to dinner with us to get a square meal – one, not having eaten for several days, actually fainted on the floor on arrival.

There was a place called La Maison Russe which was run by an Englishwoman called Dorothy Paget. It was an old people's home for Russians. I used to enjoy walking round Paris with one of the teachers called Mademoiselle Galakoff or Kira Nikolayevna as the Russians called her. She would go round seeing these old people, sometimes taking them parcels of food or old clothes. They had their samovars and icons all round them and a few small possessions that they had managed to save from Russia. The American girls never came as they didn't particularly enjoy doing that kind of thing. We were not allowed to go out on our own, and if we did, we were often teased and pestered. Being fairly large and fair, I didn't look like a French girl and boys would rush up to me and do tiresome things like pulling my suspenders and letting them go click, or shoving their hands down my front and making rude remarks, but all in good fun really. They made us giggle. When we went round together in a group looking at the various places of interest – picture galleries, churches and so on – we would probably be perhaps a dozen girls with one chaperone. We had an old French chaperone called Mme Valleton. She had an umbrella and she also wore a wig with a hat on top. We often used to get pursued by some of the male students, and as they rushed about shouting things at us she would attack them with her umbrella, with the result that her hat used to go very much askew and her wig almost came off.

I did not learn a great deal of French because the other girls were all American or British – so we spoke mostly English amongst ourselves – and the staff were mainly Russian, although we were supposed to speak French all the time. After six months I was sent down to Bordeaux to a French family and there I had to speak nothing but French as nobody else spoke English. I think I learnt more during that month than I did the whole of the rest of time. However, even if I didn't learn much in the way of the language I did learn other things – it was good for me seeing all the old pictures, churches, historic buildings and meeting the French people as well as Russians and Americans. We also had dancing lessons with a funny old man who used to try and instruct us, but I don't think he taught us very much as he was very old and doddery. I also learnt a little about clothes from my American schoolmates.

After my year in France I was brought back to England and sent to a domestic science college. This was a completely different life. The college was in Devonshire in a very rural area. We learnt cooking, sewing and laundry. I enjoyed this because my friends from home, the Dudgeon twins, were there. They were a year ahead of me but I was able to share a bedroom with one of them. Apart from that I liked cooking and sewing. The whole course lasted three terms, ending in a diploma. But again my parents saw no point in my taking exams and they decided two terms were sufficient. They thought I would learn quite enough about cooking and sewing in that time and save expense.

One summer, when I was about seventeen, we were lent a cottage at Cliveden by Lord and Lady Astor. They were not really my uncle and aunt but we always called them Aunt Nancy and Uncle Waldorf because our Astor cousins did. They were always very kind to us. Aunt Nancy, who was the first woman to take her seat in Parliament, seemed somewhat eccentric to us children. She was a Christian Scientist, a teetotaller and very outspoken. She would say – and usually shout – whatever she felt. But though she might have been frightening to some, she never frightened me and she was always very kind to me.

We stayed for a month or two at this cottage. It was close to the stud with the mares and foals grazing outside, and we could go in and look at the horses whenever we fancied. It was a great country for bicycling and we rode our bicycles all over the place. There was also the River Thames to swim in and a boat house containing several boats which we could play with. We became quite proficient at rowing and paddling and sometimes we would row as far as Marlow and Maidenhead. We used to swim across the river and back though we had to watch out when setting off in case there was a boat coming down the river full of trippers. It was an idyllic summer and we were very happy. Later on I spent one or two weekends at Cliveden staying there for house parties. There were several Astor boys, two about the same age as myself, and they sometimes had teenage parties. I don't think I was a social success because I didn't know the people well and they had known each other for years. There were many Cavendishes, Cecils, Astors and Pagets, so I was rather an outsider. All kinds of people stayed at Cliveden. Once there were some Chinese, who we were told were robber barons; at the same time there were twenty-two schoolboy cricketers staying in the house. Aunt Nancy was rather put out when one of the Chinese asked if they were all her son Bill's brothers.

In the spring of 1934, when I was almost eighteen, I had to 'come out' in London. My mother was ill and unable to cope with me so I went to stay at Carlton House Terrace with my Aunt Vi. She was very busy and could not do everything for me, so various other aunts took me round shopping to buy suitable clothes. When I had acquired what they judged a 'suitable outfit', I proceeded to 'do the Season', as it was called. In those days all the girls of about seventeen or eighteen who were to come out were written down on a list. The parents of each were supposed to give a dance. Once you were on the list, you were invited to all the other girls' dances and in turn you invited them all back to yours. Aunt Vi very kindly gave a dance for me. In fact Aunt Vi and Uncle John gave a ball every year for some reason or other, and this particular year their ball was just called my coming out dance. The girls were all chaperoned and usually attended the dances with their mothers, who sat there all night and watched – unless they happened to find someone's father to dance with. At the end of the evening they would escort their daughters home. As my mother was unable to do this, a maid was engaged for me and I was allowed to go to the dances by myself in a taxi and then later the maid would come and bring me home. I was not allowed to come home alone at two or three in the morning.

I was very unsophisticated and had not been to dances before. I didn't know how you got a partner, how long you stayed with him, or anything. Each girl had a programme with the dance numbers on it and as you were asked for a dance you filled in the man's name against the dance number.

There was a card on the piano to show what was the number of the dance. My card was often fairly empty.

Fortunately, before my first dance I went to dinner with some friends from Kenya, the Freddie Wards and their daughter Sheila who was a little older than me. It was a small dinner party, only about four or six people, and when we went on to the dance I danced with the two men who were in our party. Then a footman came and said to me 'Your maid is waiting for you.' I was so glad to get away from this awful ordeal that I flung myself out of the arms of the man with whom I was dancing and fled downstairs to the ladies' cloakroom where I found my maid and home we went. My poor partner must have been rather astonished.

People gave dinner parties before dances and invited so many men and girls. I had no mother around, so I had to attend the dinner parties alone and I went through torture sometimes wondering whether I was going to the right place. I never seemed to know the people with whom I was dining. In fact I didn't really know anyone in London. It was usual, if you were giving a dinner party for a dance, to put a red carpet outside the entrance door; often in Eaton Square you would find several red carpets in front of different doors. I used to clutch my invitation card and check very carefully that I was going through the right door. It was my nightmare that one day I might go into the wrong house and be thrown out.

Frequently I would arrive in the hall to be announced and find that I didn't know a single soul there and I wondered desperately whether I *had* after all come through the right door. I suppose this was good for me; at least it made me self-reliant. At one dance I was delighted to meet someone I knew, Eddie Sladen, our next-door neighbour in Kenya. He was in London on a course of some sort. He was excited because he had just got a car and asked whether I would like to come and look at it. I thought this a good idea and we went down the street to where it was parked. I don't suppose we were out for more than ten minutes. However, someone must have told my aunt, for the next day I was given a terrible scolding and was told that I had ruined my reputation and I was never to go out into the street like that with a young man again.

Some of the balls were really beautiful. They took place in embassies or other lovely houses. The people at these balls were not all young girls like me but people of all ages. Some of the ladies wore the most exquisite jewels and dresses and the houses were filled with priceless pictures and *objets d'art*. And although I didn't have much fun as far as the dancing was concerned, because I knew few people and was very shy, I really did enjoy seeing sights which I suppose I shall never see again.

When the time came for my presentation at Court, my mother was still not well, and it was arranged that my Aunt Ruby Cromer should present me. The custom was that girls had to be presented by somebody who had herself been presented both on her coming out and on her marriage. My Aunt Ruby was married to Rowland Cromer, who happened to be the Lord Chamberlain and my grandmother was lady-in-waiting to Queen Mary. So I had what was known as the Royal Entree. I was dressed up at Carlton House Terrace in the regulation finery – in my case a light ivory-coloured satin dress with a long train and white gloves which reached above my elbows and three ostrich feathers in my hair. When I was ready I was paraded before all the household which again was the custom, then a royal carriage arrived for me from Buckingham Palace Mews. It was a closed carriage pulled by two horses with a coachman in front in full livery and top hat. I was driven all the way from Carlton House Terrace to Chelsea Park Gardens where my grandmother lived. It was quite a way and whenever we stopped at a traffic block, people would peer in the windows and say 'Who's that? Oh, nobody important.' At Chelsea Park Gardens I was joined by my grandmother and then we drove back to Buckingham Palace.

Most other girls and their mothers had to queue up in the Mall in their motor cars before being let into the Palace, but as we had the Royal Entree we just drove up to the Palace in the carriage. My grandmother announced that she had to join Queen Mary, so I was given into the charge of a page. He was a type of footman in a red coat, but an elderly man, not a boy as you might imagine. I was taken along miles and miles of passage with red carpet until I eventually reached my Uncle Rowland's offices. There I met my Aunt Ruby who took me to the Throne Room, where we had to sit and wait until our turn came. There were other people such as ambassadors' wives to be presented as well, but as we had the Entree we came first. This made it rather nerve-racking for me. There were no other young girls with us and I could not see what people were doing and I was terrified. I had been told to make two curtsies, one to the Queen and one to the King as I went past. I thought I'd make an awful bosh of this. My grandmother was standing next to the Queen, eyeing me and I expect saying 'That's my granddaughter'. However, I managed quite well and then we were back in our seats and I was able to sit and watch all the other debutantes go by with their mothers. One by one they filed past, made their curtsies and passed on through into another room. It all went off smoothly; nothing terrible happened, as I had thought it might.

One way and another the Season was quite amusing. My mother had a flat near Marble Arch but spent most of her time there in bed. She must already have been suffering from cancer by then, though we were shielded from the truth. I used to visit her every day and tell her what was going on. When the Season finished, I went to stay with my grandmother at Hydon, and she took me to Ascot. She and I went alone; we had no party. I was all dressed up for the occasion in a long grey organza dress with a pink and green sash and huge picture hat. Off we set and when we arrived made our way to the Royal Household Stand. My grandmother told me she had been asked by Queen Mary to look out for the Prince of Wales (later Edward VIII) and Mrs Wallace Simpson, but she decided it was no good her following them to see what they were up to because they would recognize her immediately. They did not know me, so I had to do it. I climbed to the very top of the Royal Household Stand and there I saw them sitting side by side, so I took up a seat a few rows behind and was able to come down later and report to my grandmother that they were there.

After the Season I went up to Scotland and stayed with various people for a few weeks. My father then came to England for a holiday and to see my mother and at the end of the year it was arranged for us all to go back to Kenya. A passage was booked for me on a Dutch boat to travel back with Muriel and Jex Blake and their daughter Daphne; and so eventually by the end of 1934 I found myself back in Kenya – and very very pleased to be there.

PART III

Learning to Farm

1
Calves and Ticks

When I came home from England in 1934, I had no idea what I was going to do. I hadn't been trained for any kind of job. I was given an old second-hand Chevrolet box-body car which had cost £30 and there was a young mare I was told I could have as my own. She was the daughter of my beloved old pony Paulette by a thoroughbred stallion.

The three Dudgeon girls had also come home. They had completed their domestic science courses and had been presented at Court, but they had not done the Season as I had. Geraldine Sladen was also back; she had done an art course. Her father had died some years before and her mother had remarried. They had sold the farm, Fintry, next to us and had gone to live at Elburgon about ten miles away. So we were all living close to each other and able to do things together as before. Nowadays it would seem strange that none of us thought of getting any kind of job; none of us had well-off parents. I suppose we all thought we would enjoy ourselves for a few years till we found suitable husbands; then we would get married and bring up a family.

My father gave me an allowance of 100 shillings a month and I think the other girls had something similar. We enjoyed ourselves though. We would go to each other's houses and sew and talk and ride. At weekends we would usually go to polo. Most farmers had a few ponies which they used for farm work during the week and to play polo at weekends. Sometimes there were polo tournaments and often dances on Saturday evenings. I had my car and so was mobile. Geraldine also had a car so we were able to go where we liked.

After I had been back about four months, my father announced that all he was doing on the farm was losing money. He would have to give the European manager notice to leave. He had brought some 'grade cows' (that is native crossed with exotic) to see how they would do; and he asked me if I would like the job of looking after them, supervising the milking, the calf rearing and so on. We also had a small amount of agriculture because we had to grow rations for the labour as well as stock feed and next I was asked if I would mind looking after this too. My father at that time spent most of his time in Nairobi and only used to come home at weekends. He had always employed a manager before. Now I was to be manager. I thought this would be an interesting challenge and I agreed. I was eighteen; I never dreamt that running the farm would be my occupation for the next forty-five years!

I had always had it impressed on me that, as a European in Africa, I would have to be a leader and take responsibility, and I must behave so as to earn the respect of the people amongst whom I lived. So it did not seem at all strange to me, that I, as an ignorant eighteen-year-old girl, should be given charge of 3,500 acres of Africa, and power to rule over about thirty African families. I realize now how much I was helped and guided by the Africans in senior positions – though perhaps sometimes more to their advantage than to mine. My father told me that he wanted me to pay for all the running of the farm out of the cream cheque from the cows, which would be our only income. I was also to pay for all the household expenses and my own monthly allowance. He said he still had enough income from his few overseas investments, pension, etc. to pay for his and my mother's personal expenses and Loder's wages. He thought if we lived carefully we would be able to manage.

My father was a man of very simple tastes. He had little aesthetic appreciation and was quite happy living in any kind of surroundings; he liked simple food and he rarely drank anything more than one whisky and water as a sundowner each evening. He hated buying new clothes and what he wore was usually old and patched. He was what is called a 'good mixer' and he was quite at ease with people from any walk of life. He had been brought up amongst grooms and keepers, as well as dukes and millionaires, and had served in the Army; he could fit in with anyone. He was over six feet tall with fair hair and twinkling blue eyes and a rather long pointed nose. Since he had been wounded he stooped and used two sticks to help him walk. He had a quick brain but was intolerant of others who were slower or who took a different point of view. 'You're an idiot' he would shout at a lady who was partnering him at bridge when she made a mistake. 'You're a damn fool of a woman' he would yell at me if I did something he didn't like – at the same time making a lunge at me with one of his sticks. This sometimes upset people who didn't know his ways but he was the kindest of men. He loved a party and dancing and pretty girls right up to his old age. As a young man he had been a natural ball games player. After he was wounded he couldn't play as before, but until his arthritis became too bad he still loved golf, croquet and polo. He was a very amusing teller of stories, often scurrilous, and would roar with laughter when telling them. I now regret that I had no tape recorder when he was alive – as so many of his stories I have forgotten.

My mother was quite different. She was small and delicate, had dark hair and green eyes, and was beautiful, gracious and gentle. She loved theatricals and drama and reading poetry, in French and German as well as English. She enjoyed listening to music like Strauss waltzes or Gilbert and Sullivan, although she was not musical herself. She was completely unpractical and I doubt whether she had ever sewn on a button or boiled an egg in her life – or for that matter even washed her own hair. She had a wonderful sense of humour and could always see the amusing side of things. She used to say that she was never bored. She liked to be surrounded by beauty and comfort and wear lovely clothes. I think that she was always conscious of coming from a different background from most people in Kenya, where there were very few people with whom she had much in common. She missed her mother and her sisters and other friends in England very much. When our money began to get less and less, and we had to make economies, it was a real hardship for her, and she began to suffer from acute depression and insomnia. Eventually her health broke down altogether. She had never been very strong and she died in England in 1938 after an operation for cancer and was buried at Minto. My father told me after she had died that he was afraid that he had done a cruel thing when he brought her to live in Africa.

Now I must tell you more about the farm. It was 3,500 acres and lay among the foothills of a volcano called Londiani (meaning 'bamboo' in Masai). On the eastern side, the lower end of the farm ran along the Molo river, which was our only permanent water supply. On the southern side was what had been the Sladens' farm. After General Sladen died it had been sold to some people called Kuester who had come from Breslau in East Germany to escape the Nazis. A forest reserve was to the west and on the northern side was Gogar, the Dudgeons' farm. The elevation went from about 6,000 feet above sea level at the lower end by the river and up to 7,500 feet on the western boundary where it met the forest reserve. This was a distance of about four miles, the width of the farm being about three-quarters of a mile; it was rectangular in shape.

We had our large stone house with the mud and wattle guest house and the old mud and wattle huts were still standing. We also had some mud and wattle stables and a manager's house built in the same material, all with thatched roofs. A little way off were the farm buildings which consisted of a ration store, an office and a small workshop. We had at that time a Sikh carpenter, who kept the wagons in order and he had his small mud and wattle house as well. Then there was what was known as the 'camp' which was about twenty round mud and thatched huts for the casual labour. The Kikuyu squatters' houses were spread all over the farm.

There were three or four hundred acres of old maize fields, but they had been abandoned and allowed to grow weeds and couch grass. They were exhausted after growing many crops of maize without any fertilizer and had been ploughed up and down hill in straight lines regardless of the contours and consequently were badly eroded. About seventy acres were fenced, which was where the grade cattle were kept. Apart from this there was no fencing on the farm. There were no dams or pumped water, no piping for irrigation or for drinking. In 1934, just before I came back from England, my father had had a borehole dug. It was about 350 feet deep but it only gave about 75 gallons of water an hour which was barely enough for our use in the house. Except for the areas which had been planted to maize, the rest of the farm was covered with fairly thick *leleshwa* bush and in some parts acacia, cedar and olive forest.

We had quite a number of work oxen and some machinery suitable for use with oxen, such as ploughs, harrows, and so on. There was one old McCormick Deering tractor with iron wheels that ran on petrol and power kerosene, a small engine which powered the borehole and an electric light generator at the house, but no other machinery. There was a cattle dip near the river which had to be filled with an arsenic solution. My father had sold the native cattle that we had previously kept for the house milk and also a good many work oxen and it was with this money that he bought the new 'grade cows'.

In the early days my father had persuaded various experts, so called, to come and advise him. They probably didn't know very much themselves. He was told that fruit would grow very well around here, so he imported 250 fruit trees from South Africa – apples, oranges, plums, citrus and others. But fruit trees are no use in this part of Kenya. It is too hot for apples and plums and the citrus need a lot of water for irrigation which we did not have; so that was a failure. The caterpillars ate the flax and the price dropped right down so that too was a failure. He then started growing maize which was fairly successful, except that it was eaten by cutworm. In those days little was known about pests and diseases. A young Scotsman who had been taken on as manager proved to be unreliable. He broke the tractor through carelessness, and overstayed his leave by two days, leaving the labour without rations. Over a hundred of them had to go to bed without food one night.

I soon realized that I had a tremendous amount to learn about running a farm. One of our former managers had a herd of Ayrshire cows at Elburgon, about eight miles away, and I used to go up there and he taught me the rudiments of milk production and calf rearing. We soon bought a non-pedigree bull from him. My father had decided that we should keep Ayrshire cows as they were strong, hardy animals and he thought they would do well on our rough land. He had not previously kept cattle on a commercial basis. But it soon became clear that it would have to be a dairy farm and I had to learn about animal husbandry, absolutely from scratch. I knew nothing about it, even though I had been brought up on the farm. In those days the veterinary services were negligible. There was only one Government vet in Nakuru (eighteen miles and in those days several hours away), so you had to do practically all your own veterinary work. I had to learn how to inoculate subcutaneously, intramuscularly and intravenously. I had to learn to carry out a post-mortem and be able to diagnose what disease an animal had died from. I had to take blood, gland and spleen smears and send these smears into the veterinary office in Nakuru for diagnosis. Once the disease had been identified, it might be possible to combat it, but often the answer would come back N.P.S. which meant 'no parasite seen'. Then I wouldn't know what to do. It was before antibiotics and there weren't very many drugs that could be used.

Our chief enemy was the tick. We had to dip the cattle every five days in an arsenic solution which had to be mixed in exactly the right proportions. If too strong the animals got burnt and their skins would get very sore, which put back the milk production. If it were too weak, it didn't kill the ticks. There were several types of ticks – brown ticks, blue ticks and variegated ticks – and they each had their special places where they liked attaching themselves to a cow. Some of them had one life span, others had different stages during their lifetime, like caterpillars. I had to learn which kind of ticks spread which disease and what their habits were. Some of them would get under the tails and in the ears; some would get on the necks, others in between the cleft of hooves and others into the switch of their tails. So I had to make constant and careful inspections to ensure that the cattle had no ticks on any part of them. Then, of course, apart from tick-borne diseases there were others such as blackwater, anthrax, rinderpest, pleuro-pneumonia, brucellosis and mastitis. It was very disheartening, when you had saved up to buy some cows, had got them heavy in calf and then noticed one day one of them standing apart from the others, not eating, her ears drooping, her breathing laboured, her flanks heaving and her hair standing on end. You would know she was sick and you had to try and find out what was wrong by looking in her eyes, examining her gums, taking her temperature, feeling her glands to see if they were swollen. After a while you became fairly experienced at diagnosing which disease a cow was suffering from and then you only had to send the smears to Nakuru for confirmation. But there were many diseases which could not be identified. I can't say how discouraging it was when there was first one sick, then next day a few more and you were left wondering how many more would get sick and die.

Then I had to learn to brand and castrate calves and de-horn them. We de-horned all our cattle. This was fairly simple; you merely cut off the horn bud with a sharp knife and then applied a red hot iron, a piece of flat iron, an old spring or some such thing, then covered it with cow dung. This was the local way of de-horning and it proved quite effective. When we were castrating, which was done with a knife, the herdsmen would sometimes put the testicles onto the fire and then eat them. And when you had removed the engorged ticks the children used to pop them into their mouths and eat the blood. I found this rather repulsive but after all it was only cow's blood.

There was a time when several of our herdsmen became sick and complained of bad backs. One young Masai in particular was very bad so I took him to the doctor in Nakuru but he was unable to diagnose the trouble. Then I took him to Nairobi to a back specialist who immediately diagnosed brucellosis. He must have caught it from drinking the milk on the farm. However the specialist told me to take him to the ladies' lingerie shop and get him fitted with a corset. I felt rather embarrassed at the thought of taking a Masai, almost naked and smeared in red mud, into a smart ladies' lingerie shop and asking them to fit him with a corset. The doctor told me not to be so stupid so off I went. Fortunately I met a friend, a man who said that he had always longed to enter that particular shop, and he would come too. To our surprise, the young European shop assistant didn't turn a hair at having to measure my Masai for a corset. The corset, together with medication, proved effective and eventually he was cured. Getting our cattle cleared of brucellosis was another story.

Then I had to deal with calving problems. I had to learn to push the calf back into the mother and turn it if it was in the wrong position, or pull out its front legs and get them straight so it could be born. We used to have to tie ropes to the calf's legs sometimes and around the mouth to pull it out when it got stuck. Sometimes the cow retained the after-birth, which had to be removed – a nasty, messy job. Successive vets were very kind in showing me how to do all these things and gradually I learnt by experience. I was rather amazed once when staying with a farmer in England I heard him ring for the vet to help him to replace a ring in a bull's nose. It seemed extraordinary to me that anyone had to ask a vet to come for such a simple task. I also had to learn about milk production and the feeding and rearing of the calves.

We didn't have many cows to start with, only about twenty, but whenever we could get enough money together we would buy a few more and gradually built up the herd. There were 1,700 when I gave up the farm, 350 in milk. I had to be careful when buying cattle not to bring in any kind of sickness. I had to make sure that they were in calf and that they hadn't any breeding diseases. Gradually our herd expanded. We bought more bulls, sticking to the Ayrshire breed, and after a time we were milking cows that we had reared as calves.

We had to record the milk production very carefully, because although we gave our herdsmen a generous milk ration they were always apt to steal any extra that they could. Sometimes they would hide a gourd in the grass near the milking place and tip some in when no one was looking, or they would just drink it there and then whilst milking; sometimes they would milk the cows at night. Each cow was marked with a number and her milk production carefully recorded by a clerk. At first we sold nothing but cream because there was no market for liquid milk. We had to separate the cream ourselves. We had portable dairies out in the fields which were moved around by oxen from place to place every few days. The separators were also in the field in portable separator houses and were turned by hand. The cream would be loaded onto donkeys in panniers and taken to the railway station in Rongai, where it was consigned to the creamery, about seventy miles away. All the other farmers around were doing the same, so people took great interest at the railway station in seeing how many cans so and so was bringing; there was a certain amount of rivalry about this. The creamery would send you a receipt with the weight of cream and the butterfat percentage written on it. You had then to compare the amount the creamery had credited you for with the amount you had estimated you should have had from the milking records and see if they tallied. As can be imagined, there were many opportunities for slips to occur between cow and creamery. You had to be forever vigilant and spend many hours at the dairy while the cows were being milked.

Not only was milk stolen but cows themselves would disappear occasionally. All our cattle were supposed to be counted daily, and I would count them personally once a month. They were all marked with an individual number, each calf getting a number as soon as it was born. But they went. The most usual way to steal a heifer was not to record when a cow had her calf. Then there was an extra calf in the calf herd. Then the thief would take a large calf and put it in the weaner herd, and then take a larger weaner and put it with the heifers and then he was able to take a nice heifer home one night. Sometimes there would be a raid and you would find a whole group of animals had gone. Once forty-six of our Ayrshire heifers disappeared in the night and I found them about twenty miles away next morning. I think the thieves had been unable to reach their hideout before light and so had just abandoned them. It was amazing how far thieves could drive cattle in just one night. I have heard of cattle going seventy miles by the morning. My cattle-raiding ancestors would have been proud of that, but not of the methods used. Often the cattle would be in a terrible state, having been goaded with knives to make them move faster.

We had a problem with the skimmed milk. Most of the skim milk would go to the labour for their rations but after a while we had too much for this and so we decided to start keeping pigs. My father's friend Mervyn Ridley very kindly gave us a black gilt, Mary. I had her built a little house and looked after her carefully. I thought in my ignorance that the fatter a pig was the better, so we gave her plenty of food and in time she became very fat. When the time came for her to breed, I arranged with a neighbour, who had a boar, for her to be mated and told one of the herdsmen to drive her over. I didn't realize then that pigs have no ventilation system and cannot sweat. They let the heat out through their mouths and if a pig gets very hot it blows up. My very fat gilt was driven along in the heat of the day and in the hot sun she got apoplexy and lay down and died.

Later I acquired some more pigs and had to think where to keep them. The old manager's house was mud and wattle but had cement floors and so I decided this would be a good home for the pigs. It didn't take them long to knock it down but by that time I had managed to build a stone pigsty. We had by then about forty sows and their followers. I went in for pedigree Landrace and did quite well showing them, winning a number of prizes.

There were many other aspects of farming which I had to learn besides the animals. There were the accounts; my kind neighbour Major Dudgeon taught me how to do double entry and draw up a trial balance. I had to learn about building; we had plenty of stone on the farm and were able to cut stone in a quarry. We built simple stone buildings with corrugated iron roofs. This involved learning to mix cement and the different thicknesses of stone. I was able to get African contractors to do this work but had to supervise them fairly closely. I had also to learn about water. We had a few springs on the farm, though none permanent, but we had several good situations for making dams. I had a small level and I learnt how to take levels and made dams using the work oxen and dam scoops. Each scoop was pulled by about six oxen. They would pull the earth along in the scoops and heap it up in a bank and then walk back across it. In time you scooped out the ground and built it up into a dam bank. The walking over by the oxen consolidated it and made it very hard. Then you took levels to see if the top was level and measured how far back the water would go and then made a spillway that was big enough to take all the surplus water during the heavy rains. I think making dams was one of the most satisfactory tasks I ever did on the farm. It was wonderful to wake up one morning after heavy rain and see a big sheet of water where there had previously been none.

One neighbour who gave me much advice was Hugh Barclay, who lived about ten miles away, between Rongai and Nakuru. As a young man he had served in the First World War in the Gunners. After the war he had come to Kenya to work on a coffee farm, but decided he liked stock and mixed farming better and so he had bought land near us. He married an Irish girl, Patsy Kilkelly, whose father had been a doctor with the Grenadier Guards, and had been present at the Battle of Omdurman. The land they bought was waterless and cobalt-deficient, and consisted mainly of lava ash, but in time he had converted it into a very productive farm, growing good crops of maize and wheat. He had one of the best Friesian herds in the country. Hugh was always ready to help me over problems I found difficult.

Some of our land had been terribly eroded by ploughing it up and down regardless of the contours. In the 1930s a Soil Conservation Service was formed in Kenya and I was able to get these people to come and make cut-off drains and contours on all our ploughed land and they mapped out where the roads and drainage ways should go until eventually all the lower part of the farm was contoured. We did all the work with oxen. The oxen had to have two brands, A.M. and T.A.M. meant they had been inoculated against rinderpest and T. meant they were immune to East Coast fever, a tick-borne disease that was almost 100 per cent fatal. The native cattle had a certain immunity to this; when they were calves they would contract it and sometimes recover, though not always, and then they would be immune. So you had to buy oxen where East Coast fever was endemic. They would then be put into a Government holding ground and exposed to East Coast fever infection and if they did not become sick it was assumed that they must have had it as calves and were immune. They were then branded with T. The grade cattle were not immune and if they contracted the disease it was nearly always fatal. The oxen were also used on the open roads for transport and there was a law that only those branded with T. could be used, otherwise they might spread infected ticks.

The art of using work oxen had come up from South Africa with the Dutch-descended Afrikaner people and it was a beautiful sight to watch a good team of oxen working. There were sixteen oxen in a team, to pull a three-furrow disc plough, or a wagon which was loaded with about thirty-two 100 lb. sacks. You would try and match your team so that they were all red or all black or all mixed. In the morning a well-trained team would be driven to the yoking-in place. The yokes and chains were laid along the ground in a line and the oxen would know their places. Each ox would go to his own place and stand there with his head down ready to be yoked in. The drivers had long sticks with looped reims – or straps – on them which served as whips. You always made your driver loop the reim, because if they had a loose reim it could flick out a bit of flesh or even an eye if badly used. But a good driver rarely hit an ox. The whole system of using work oxen was simple and practical; it had to be for the Afrikaner people, as they were often far from outside help, away in the bush. The yokes were made out of sapling trees pierced at each end with holes, through which went the skey, which was a large peg, thicker at one end than the other. This went either side of the bullock's neck and underneath was a twisted bit of reim called a 'strop', which ran from one of these skeys to the other and formed a neck strap. The yokes lay on the bullocks' necks and underneath went the strop. The yoke had an iron ring in the middle which was attached to the chain and the oxen would be yoked in two by two. In front of the team a boy would walk with a long reim attached to the horns of the leading pair and he would hold this in his hands behind his back and lead them to show the way. But very often well-trained oxen did not need this.

The oxen would obey the commands of the driver; he would say '*kom*' for them to turn, and '*ano*' for them to stop and '*turi*' when he wanted them to move backwards. These were corruptions of Afrikaans words. Some of the drivers were good, some not so good, but I don't think any of them were nearly as good as the Afrikaner people themselves. The wagons also could be more or less home-made. The only complicated parts were the axle, the hubs and the brakes, which were made of metal.

The wheels had wooden spokes and iron tyres about four inches wide. When it became very dry the spokes and other wooden parts shrank and the spokes might fall out, so the wheels had to be soaked in the river. We had an Indian *fundi* who could make and repair the wheels. The axles had to be greased and that was part of the driver's duties. We also had smaller carts called Scotch carts, for which only eight oxen were needed. Then there were cultivators which were pulled by a pair of oxen; the yoke for these was much wider to span the rows of maize for weeding purposes. The reims were made out of cow hides cut into strips and soaked in water and hung up with heavy weights to stretch them. A man would stick a pole through the reims as they were hanging and would walk round and round twisting them; they had to be constantly rubbed with oil.

We had an old tractor but only used it for stationary work. It had a pulley which drove a belt for shelling the maize cobs and it was also used to grind maize meal for the Africans' rations. We didn't grow very many crops, only enough maize for the labour rations and the cattle and pig feed, and also some barley, which was fed to the pigs to make a balanced diet with the skim milk. When the pigs reached about 200 lb. we would take them down to Rongai in an ox-cart and put them on the train. There was a special pig train which went once a week and everybody had to mark their pigs with an identity mark. Then they went off in little compartments on the train to Uplands, the bacon factory, where they would be slaughtered and graded.

I always hated machinery; I thought it ugly, dirty, noisy and smelly. It pinched your fingers, broke your nails, covered you with oil. When it went wrong, it was a terrible expense to buy a spare part. You have to feed it expensive petrol and it produces no manure; it doesn't breed and you can't eat it. So I didn't use it more than I had to.

Another art I had to learn was fencing. It was not much use trying to improve the pasture unless you had fencing. We had very little fencing when I started running the farm and gradually we had to extend this until the whole farm was fenced. I had to learn about fence posts, depth of holes, corner posts, distances between posts and all the many different ways of fencing. The most economical and practical way had to be found and we were fortunate as we had cedar trees on the farm which we were able to use as fence posts. We used *leleshwa* for droppers – intermediate light posts – to keep the wires apart. *Leleshwa* (tarcanthus) is a grey bush that used to grow all over the farm. It was inedible for the cattle and useless except for droppers and firewood. The roots particularly made very good firewood but were knobbly and difficult to use as fuel on the railway, so they were not very practical except for domestic fires.

One of the problems on the farm was thick bush. We had to dig out the *leleshwa* by the roots and unless you removed the entire root it would spring up again. We used crowbars for this and piled the roots up into heaps. Sometimes we paid the clearers by the acre, sometimes by the cubic feet of roots they had unearthed. Another problem was the acacias. I have identified eight different types of acacia on the farm and I think anyone more expert could probably find others. Some of these acacias were easier to dig out than others, but some of them were like couch grass; they had long lateral roots which sprang up as much as thirty feet away from the original tree and we found it very difficult to remove all these roots unless we ploughed the entire field. If we ploughed the field, we broke a good many ploughshares in the process. Later we tried herbicides and many different ways of applying them – spraying, drilling and even painting on the stumps. But although some died, others would go dormant, sometimes for as long as a year or two, and then they would spring up again. Many of the areas on the farm were impossible to plough, the land being steep, hilly or rocky. Eventually we found that the best way of dealing with thorn trees was to prune them, removing the lower branches; the trees then continued to grow and formed a canopy under which grass would still grow.

We also had some forest on the farm and were able to use the trees for timber for building. We employed pitsawyers, who dug a pit and erected a kind of stand which they called an *ndege* meaning 'bird'. They would then lay the tree on this and saw it up into planks, one man in the pit bottom, another on the top. Some of the trees were no use for anything except firewood and had to be cleared out and thinned before we could use the land for crops or grazing. Much of this timber we cut, stacked and sold to the railway for fuel. In those days the railway would always buy wood for their engines. As we were not very far from the line, we made quite a bit of money selling firewood. All the money we made, a little bit here and there, went back into the farm, to buy more stock or fencing wire, or to put up more buildings.

2

The People on the Farm

When I started running the farm we had three main tribes of Africans working for us. We had Luo, Kikuyu and Masai. I use the word tribe because that is the word Europeans used in those days. Nowadays, I know, many Africans object to the use of the word. They say that in the dictionary the meaning given is 'a collection of primitive people', and they do not like being called primitive. But we used the word to mean a group of people who spoke the same language, wore the same type of clothing and had the same kind of customs. I don't know a better word. I realize now that the tribes were not so well defined as we thought. There was some mixing; but in general they used to take pride in whichever kind of people they were and would object to being classed with anybody else. We also had two types of labour, those called 'casuals' and others called 'squatters' or 'resident labour'. The Kikuyu were all squatters, the Masai and the Luo were all casual. The squatters had come with their families and their stock to settle on our farm and had a contract with us to stay on the farm and work six 'tickets' of thirty days per year for us. They were allowed to cultivate a holding and to keep their own sheep and goats on the farm. The casuals were engaged month by month; they did not cultivate land or keep stock.

Every male African had to carry an identification certificate which was known as a *kipande* which means 'a piece of something'. These were bits of paper that could be folded up and put in a tin box which had a hole in the top. They could put a string through the hole and hang it round their necks. On these bits of paper were recorded the name of the man, his father's name, his tribe, his location and his age group and it was numbered and marked with his thumb print. When you took a man on, you filled in your own name as employer, the rate of pay and the nature of the man's work and there were columns for when he left, and the signature of the employer. This could become a very good reference. If a man had only a few entries and had started at a low rate and after some time had ended with a higher, it was obvious that he was a good reliable man. If on the other hand, there were numerous entries at low pay you knew what to expect. Later on, there was much political agitation against these *kipandes*, partly because of the thumb print. Most people in those days couldn't write so the only way they could identify themselves was by the thumb print – but it began to be thought derogatory. Of course, the system could be abused: an employer might unjustly refuse to sign people off when they wanted to leave and as an African could not get another job until this was done he was forced to stay. It was only the African men who had to carry these *kipandes*; they were obliged to carry them at all times as they had to show them when asked to do so by a policeman or anyone in authority, or even a farmer who wished to know what a stranger was doing on his land. They were abolished in the end, and all men, whoever they were, had to carry identification cards with their thumb prints on them. Now it was the turn of the Europeans to object, because they were not illiterate. Why should they make thumb prints? However, the Government insisted that they could not differentiate by race and as some people could not write everyone must give their thumb print. Nowadays, everyone, both men and women, have identity cards, still with thumb prints.

When we engaged a man, we gave him what was known as a ticket; this was a card that was divided into thirty squares and gave his name, his *kipande* number and his rate of pay. He made a contract to work for thirty days and these thirty days were supposed to be worked within the next forty-two days. Each day you ticked the man's card when he had finished his work. He would then receive his rations. If he didn't work then the ticket was not marked and no rations. A man was not due his pay until he had completed his ticket and as people started their tickets on different days their pay became due on different days. It was impossible to pay out every day, so there would be a pay day on the farm once a month and everyone would be paid together. This meant that some people had already finished one ticket and had started another but were not entitled to pay on the new ticket until it was finished. This was another way unscrupulous employers were able to keep people working for them longer than they wanted, because the men always had extra days owing to them and the employer could refuse to pay until pay day, by which time they had started another ticket.

Some Africans liked saving up their pay; they had their rations and did not want to be paid every month. They preferred to save and then maybe when they had six tickets owing to them, cash them in at once so as to have a lump sum. I had one man who would never take his pay, so eventually I had to open a post office savings account for him and put his wages in that. Others liked to share; two men on the same rate of pay would arrange for one man to take both pays for one month and the other would go without until the following month, when he would collect both pays. We had to keep a muster roll recording all the names of employees, their *kipande* numbers, their rates of pay, the days they worked, when they were engaged, when they were discharged and when they were away sick or went on leave. The Labour Department would come and compare this with the tickets; there were no trade unions in those days.

The squatters were different. By their agreements they were obliged to work for 180 days a year only. This meant six tickets, but of course, there are fifty-two Sundays in the year so that made up nearly eight months. The rest of the time they could stay at home and do what they liked. On some farms where all the labour were squatters, they would have a double labour force and everybody changed over every six months.

This was a South African system that had been brought up here by the Afrikaner people. There were some farmers, particularly among the Afrikaners, who were known as 'Kaffir farmers'. They had a great many squatters on their farms who kept stock and had to come out to work only when asked; they received no pay. The farmer would grow some wheat or maize and the men would come out to help him plant and then there would be nothing to do but weeding, until harvest. They would just do these short periods of work and usually be quite happy to have little or no pay. They might supply milk for the household as well. This was very bad farming as it meant that nearly the whole farm was being cultivated and grazed by African squatters with no thought of development or the future. It was much frowned upon and was in fact made illegal.

Squatters received no rations, but the casuals received two pounds of maize meal, known as *posho*, a day and a small tin of coarse salt once a week. That was all that they were entitled to. At Deloraine, the Masai who worked at the dairy with the cattle had a ration of skim milk, probably up to a gallon a day a head. The maize meal that the Luo got wasn't all consumed by them; they used to feed some of it to their chickens, and I had little doubt they used to make some of it into *pombe* (beer). The Africans used to pick vegetables in the bush, wild spinach and so on, so that they had a more varied diet than this suggests. Sometimes they would be given a meat ration, and when there was sufficient skim milk they got that too.

In those days the casual labourer or ordinary worker would be paid 12 shillings per ticket and a squatter 8 shillings. Nowadays people raise their hands in horror at what they consider slave wages but the value of money was very different then. A prime steer ready for the butcher was worth 70 shillings and a rather inferior one could be had for 30 shillings. Dairy cows, the very best that could be found in the country, cost 150 to 250 shillings. A bag of maize was 3 shillings and 50 cents including the sack. A farm manager might earn 400 shillings a month, an assistant manager was lucky if he got 200. The squatters had their cultivation and their sheep and goats to live on. If you ask people nowadays how badly off they were in those days, they often say they were much better off then than they are now. They hadn't much expense in the way of clothing, and no school fees to pay.

Medical facilities were meagre. We used to have a sick parade every day and treat anybody who had anything wrong. Usually this was just coughs, colds, sores and minor ailments; but sometimes more serious diseases would break out such as plague or smallpox. Then we had to get the Government medical people to come out and inoculate or vaccinate. This used to cause a certain amount of consternation as people were rather afraid of it. So we used to line everybody up and I used to try and check as best I could that all the women and children were there. Then I would stand in the front of the line and be done before anybody else to give them confidence. I remember sending a young boy to hospital with plague when we had a bad epidemic and there was smallpox at the same time. He took a long time coming back and I wondered what had happened to him. On inquiring at the hospital I found that he had contracted smallpox as well because he had been put in the isolation ward where all these infectious diseases were grouped together. He recovered from both.

Sometimes the women used to have trouble giving birth, and I used to be called to help. Usually the woman would be sitting on the floor, or on a low stone or piece of wood, and leaning back against another woman who had her arms around the expectant mother's waist and was hanging onto her while she pushed and strained. A third woman would be ready to receive the baby when it made its appearance. When it did, the cord would be cut and the placenta would be taken away and buried near the hut. Once I remember seeing the husband of a woman who had been in labour a long time breathing into her mouth. When I asked what he was trying to do, I was told that if he breathed hard enough he might be able to blow the baby out! I am not a trained midwife and was not able to be much help, but if I thought the case was serious I would take the woman to the hospital in Nakuru, which was quite a long journey. Once or twice the baby was born in the car before we got there.

Sometimes people went mad and became violent. They would have to be put in the car, tied up with ropes and held down by two other men sitting on either side of them. It was rather embarrassing to travel in this way, as the patient would usually scream at the top of his voice and people used to look at you in astonishment as you drove past. The doctors usually said it was schizophrenia and often the patients recovered. There was also quite a lot of drunkenness which led to fights. They usually fought with clubs and could give each other pretty good cracks on the head so I often had to take them to hospital for treatment. If they were obstreperous, they too had to be tied up and escorted. Once when I was about to take someone in this state in my car, another man offered me his knife and said: 'You had better take this, that man is really bad.' I thanked him, but told him I wasn't very handy with a knife and I didn't think it would be much use.

The workers lived in mud huts. They used to build their own. They were simple to build and we were lucky to have plenty of good building material on the farm. If there were enough people to do the work, a hut could be built in a day. Different tribes have different ways of building, and different customs as to what the men do and what the women do. On our farm, the women would cut the grass for thatching and carry it to the site. The men would cut the poles in the forest. Cedar poles were the best as they didn't get eaten by white ants. The site was then cleared of grass and stones and a long pole planted in the centre. Then a circle of holes would be dug round the centre pole and shorter poles planted in these. More poles would be tied in place with the bark of the *mkeu* tree (dombeya) to make a circle and others laid onto this frame to meet in the centre. These would form the rafters for the roof. Other lighter poles would then be tied onto these horizontally and the space between filled with *vitu*, or withies, and onto this the grass would be tied to form a thatched roof. Different tribes have different ways of thatching and much depends on the kind of grass used. Once the roof was ready, the mudding would start. A large and deep hole would be made and filled with water and the men would get into this and trample in it until they had plenty of soft smooth mud. Meanwhile other men would have been tying light poles and *vitu* onto the walls of the house. When all was ready the women would slap the mud onto the walls until they were completely covered in mud and then they would smooth it off, inside and out, with their fingers.

In the old days there would be no windows; people didn't like them. They said that they gave you no privacy and made it easy for thieves to get in. The doors were made of plaited *vitu*. Nowadays, they usually put wooden frames for the doors and windows and have wooden shutters and proper doors. When the mud was dry enough it would have a finishing plaster of ashes and cow dung smoothed on and the floor would be made hard with cow dung. The finished result was a warm and comfortable house built without using any nails. A fire would be lit in the centre of the floor and kept burning all the time – this made the hut smoky but kept away the bugs.

Owing to the African custom of extended families, each family had to have a number of huts to accommodate their numerous relatives, so we had to make a rule that the farm would only pay for building one hut per worker; the rest would have to be built by their own arrangements. The materials of course came from the farm. Sometimes they had six or more huts per family. Each tribe lived separately; they didn't like mixing with each other. Once some of the Kikuyu came to me and complained that the Masai were living too close to them and were seducing the Kikuyu girls at night. I asked the Masai about this and they only laughed and said 'Well, they like it.'

As I was so ignorant about farming when I started, I tried to find books to teach myself. I also looked for anthropological books about the Africans. Nowadays, if you go into a bookshop in Nairobi you will find it full of Africana books, either about the people or the wild life. But in those days very few people took much interest in African customs and you had to go into the back of the bookshop, behind the counter or into a dusty store to find such books. I wanted to know as much about the people as possible. I have always taken an interest in what they are doing and in their languages and customs. My parents could barely speak Kiswahili but they always encouraged me to try and talk the languages. My father said he thought it important that Europeans brought up in Kenya should try and understand the local people. I had always talked Kiswahili with the people on the farm but it was a poor version as it was neither their language nor mine and I had never learnt grammatical Kiswahili. I have regretted this ever since. I did ask my parents if I could take lessons but they said: 'What is the use of learning proper Kiswahili?' The people here wouldn't understand it and of what use would it ever be to you? It was much better to learn French. I might marry a diplomat; I might not live in Kenya always. And so I never did learn proper Kiswahili nor how to read or write it. Nowadays when I have to speak it at public meetings other people can speak good Kiswahili but I talk like an uneducated yokel. African children now all learn it at school; they can talk much better Kiswahili than before and they read the newspapers and listen to the

Kiswahili radio. When I was at school in Limuru we were forbidden to speak to the Africans at all, although we could all speak Kiswahili of a sort. This was because they thought that if we talked to the Africans we might order them about, asking them to do this and that for us. Later when I spent many hours in the field supervising the work, the milking, the dipping, the making of dams, and so on, I would try to pick up any information I could about the people and their habits and they were usually very ready to talk.

Violent events took place from time to time. I have had to give evidence at two murder trials. Once Bissie Dudgeon and Geraldine Sladen arrived for lunch with me looking rather shaken and asked if I knew there was a man with his throat cut lying in the drive with blood all over the place. They had stopped to make quite sure he was dead – and he was. So we informed the police on the telephone and went to see who it was. It wasn't anybody from the farm and we discovered later that he was a railway worker. It had been pay day at the station and two men had been arguing with each other over a debt. The man who was claiming the debt had chased the other down the road towards Deloraine with a knife and had eventually caught him. He was trying to knife him when the man being attacked seized his wrist and knocked his hand away and instead of being knifed himself cut his assailant's jugular vein. That at least was his story and the other could not speak! There was a large maize field nearby and we had to get everyone out to search through the maize for the murderer in case he was lurking there – but he wasn't. Later he was caught but acquitted through lack of evidence.

The second time I had to give evidence was when some people whom I employed had been fighting. They were all drunk, and I think one hit the other over the head with an iron bar. The man who had been hit came to the house for treatment, as the farm people always did when they were injured. He had a big lump and a cut over his eye which didn't look too serious, so I just applied some disinfectant and covered it with sticking plaster and off he went. It was a fairly common occurrence for people to knock each other over the head so I didn't think more of it. It wasn't till a couple of days later that I was told he was very ill and had become unconscious. I took him to hospital where he died of meningitis and the other man in the fight was charged with murder. The defence claimed that while they had been fighting the deceased had slipped and fallen down on top of a bicycle and the handle bars had injured his head. The murderer was acquitted on that.

It was a great nuisance when people made drink and got drunk and started fighting, especially just when the cows needed milking. Cows have to be milked morning and evening seven days a week. This is absolutely essential. After a big celebration, I often found some milkers unable to milk. Either they were still too drunk or they had been fighting and had hurt their hands or feet. Those who were sober had to milk the cows as best they could for those who were absent and sometimes the cows didn't get milked properly. The brewing of drink was one of our biggest problems. It was very hard to prevent it.

We had a *kiama* (council) on the farm to settle disputes amongst the people, or to discipline those who had done wrong. This consisted of three headmen, Masai, Kikuyu and Luo, three other people nominated by the labour and three more nominated by myself. Anyone found guilty had to pay a fine and the money was put into a post office savings account and used for welfare. What it was to be used for was decided by the *kiama*. In fact a number of buildings at the farm school were built out of these funds.

There were often quarrels amongst the people that had nothing to do with the farm work. Once a certain woman complained that a man had been trying to get into her house at night so she had shut it up as securely as possible; but he climbed onto the roof, made a hole in the thatch and entered like that. She had yelled for help and people had come running, so he had made his escape the same way as he had come in, but one of his shoes came off in the process and so he was easily identified. The *kiama* would deal with such cases. After the trade unions started we had to give up the *kiama* as we were no longer allowed to fine people and this made the *kiama* powerless. So we no longer had any money for welfare.

There was a time when I was told that the headmaster of the farm school was distilling drink. The usual drink they brewed is called *busa*. It is just fermented grain and fairly harmless but when it is distilled it becomes quite dangerous, almost pure alcohol, sometimes known as 'kill me quick' or *changa*. It has been known to kill people from time to time and it affects their eyesight. Everyone knew that the headmaster was brewing this stuff but nobody would take any action, not even the School Committee. So one day I went down with the school chairman and told the headmaster that I would like to inspect all the school buildings, using the excuse that I felt sure that some of them were in need of repair. Having inspected all the classrooms and teachers' rooms we arrived at the headmaster's house. We found the bathroom door was closed and when I said 'Well, what about the bathroom? – I ought to have a look at that', he said: 'Oh, no, the bathroom's all right; nothing the matter with that.' I replied that I would like to take a look all the same and when I opened the door, of course, there was his still and all his equipment. I sent the school chairman, who fortunately drove a car, to fetch the police who came and arrested the man. The Education Department only reprimanded him and he was later transferred to be headmaster of another school.

Occasionally we had trouble with witchcraft. One of the Africans would fall sick and start pining away, saying that he had been bewitched and was going to die – and if nothing was done about it he did die. Once I was able to save a man who was bewitched. He was an old Kikuyu and he went into a decline. So I mixed up in a bottle everything I could think of, power kerosene, scent, Eno's fruit salts and various other things. I corked it and wrapped it up in a piece of paper and wrote a lot of hieroglyphics on the wrapper and bound it together with string and sealing wax until it looked very impressive. I then went to his hut and told him that I had got the *dawa* (medicine) which Europeans always took when they had been bewitched. I explained that it was very potent and gave it to him to drink. Of course, when I shook it and poured it out it fizzed, having Eno's in it and this must have impressed him greatly because the next day when I asked his son how his father was he replied: 'Oh, he is quite recovered. That was very good medicine you gave him. It boiled even though it was cold, and after he had drunk it, he vomited all the spell out of him.'

Often when people suffered aches and pains they were convinced that someone had put something into their bodies by witchcraft. I recall one man who summoned a witch doctor to deal with a pain. This man took a goat's horn and inverted it on the man's stomach. The narrow end had been cut off and he sucked through this. On removing the horn he pulled out of it all kinds of things, rats' teeth, lizards' claws and other such things. The ailing man was quite convinced that these had come out of his stomach and felt much better.

Most Africans believe that the spirits of their ancestors are hovering nearby and must be kept friendly otherwise they might do harm. Often when they fell ill, they believed that their ancestors had placed a spell on them or given them the illness. Occasionally women would be accused of bewitching other women's children. I remember a woman who came rushing into the house one day and hid under the piano in the drawing-room, screaming that people said she was a witch and were after her. She begged for protection. It was no good telling Africans not to believe these things, because they did believe in them very firmly and they had a profound psychological effect on them.

We had a man working for us once who claimed that he could find out who had stolen things. He would put a blank piece of paper in a bucket of water and soon a name would appear in writing on it. He became quite famous and people, including the police, would seek his assistance in solving theft cases. One day I asked him how he did it and he said that he would show me. He took a piece of soap and wrote on the paper. When it was dry, you couldn't see anything, but when he placed it in some water it had 'Pam' written on it. I hope that not too many people were punished for crimes they had not committed because of this man. He made quite a bit of money out of his trick. Another time a bag of cash disappeared from the drawer where I had hidden it. I threatened to pay a witch doctor to put a spell on whoever had stolen it and a day or so later I found the money back again in the drawer where I had left it.

When I went away for a few days, I had to make tremendous preparations so that everything would be done properly while I was away. When I came back I would inquire anxiously if everything was all right and usually I was given the reply, accompanied by a broad grin: 'Oh yes, everything is very good, *lakini* [however] . . .'; and then would follow some frightful disaster. The bull just imported from Europe had died; somebody had left the gate open and he had got into the lucerne and he had blown up. Or the tractor had broken some vital part or somebody had been taken ill. There was always something and sometimes I felt that really it wasn't worth going away. It was as if I were pushing a cart without brakes up a hill and the moment I stopped pushing it would run back again. For twelve years I never left the farm for more than two weeks at a time.

Although we had always to guard against pilfering on the farm, we never locked anything in the house. Our house was always open and anyone could come in day or night and we never had anything stolen. Not even a silver teaspoon went missing, although food, like sugar, and tea was apt to disappear. Loder looked after that side of things so I didn't have the housework to do.

3
The Masai

The Masai looked after our cattle; they would do not other work. They did the milking, the herding and the guarding at night. They would take the cattle to the dip and do anything to do with the cattle but they would never do any form of digging or carrying. It was beneath their dignity. The Masai are pastoral people and their cattle are everything to them. They do no agriculture but live on milk and blood, which they draw from an artery in the cow's neck and mix with the milk. The milk is put in gourds, rinsed out with cows' urine which curdles it, and together with the blood makes a kind of junket which they eat. They eat meat only occasionally when they have some reason for killing an animal. Traditionally, they eat nothing but this, so are entirely dependent on their cattle. In pre-colonial days the Masai stretched from Tanganyika right up to Lake Rudolf (now Lake Turkana) in the desolate north-west. They were by far the most powerful people in what is now up-country Kenya. But like the Moslems of the coastal region, they rejected the mission teaching and so fell behind other tribes such as the Kikuyu, many of whom attended schools. If it had not been for this they would have played a much bigger part in the life of the country.

Up to the time of colonialism, being nomads, they moved about from place to place, raiding neighbouring tribes and abducting their women and children as well as their cattle and so they became very mixed genetically. There was quite a difference between various sections: the Samburu Masai from the far north kept camels as well as cattle and their language differed a little; the Warusha Masai had even had to take to agriculture – probably they had lost all their cattle at one time with disease or war. But they all called themselves Masai.

Ours were Uasin Gishu Masai and were very mixed with the Tugen and Nandi people. After various battles, they had scattered and the bad famine and outbreak of smallpox in the 1890s had dispersed them further. That was a time when all their cattle had died and they had nothing to eat.

The Masai are divided into age groups, three for men and two for women. The boys after initiation become warriors or *moran* and after a few years elders. The girls after initiation become women and get married. There are of course sub-divisions within these broad age groups. The young men used to cover their bodies with *sereka*, a red earth mixed with mutton fat, so that they appeared completely red all over. They wore a cotton cloth twisted round under their armpits and this was also rubbed with *sereka*. The warriors would twist their long hair into strands. Sometimes they wore these loose on their shoulders and other times they tied them back in a pigtail anointed with *sereka*. Their faces were marked with patterns of white or blue. They wore beads around their necks, waists and ankles and bells on their legs. When they danced they formed a circle and chanted; then one or two of them would go into the middle and leap up and down to the beat of the chanting. The girls too had a dance, rather like follow-my-leader; they followed a leader who led the song and the others would answer her. Men and women did not dance together, always separately.

Boys and girls were regarded as very much inferior to those who had been initiated and they were always longing for the day they too would become men and women. Initiation took place for the girls when they were mature enough to bear children; for the boys when they were strong enough to go on cattle raids and to live with the *moran* in a special *manyatta* or village. As soon as a girl's breasts began to develop she was considered old enough for lovemaking. They were supposed to amuse the *moran* and they lived and slept together with them. The *moran* were supposed to restrain themselves so that the girls did not become pregnant, and in fact few of them did as they were usually too immature. When the girls reached puberty and were ready for initiation, they would start dancing and singing and go round all the various people's houses. They used to have police whistles which they blew lustily and bells on their ankles. Sometimes the parents would invite me to attend the ceremonies, which included circumcision. They have to go through so many ceremonies that it takes a long time, sometimes months or even a year, to complete the whole course. It entails training in the customs of the tribe and making the young people fit to be full members. I didn't attend all these ceremonies; some are supposed to be secret, but sometimes I used to go when they had a dance. The evening before the girls' actual circumcision took place all the young men would be lined up and would dance; and then the girls would be brought into the middle by the young men who danced round them. Sometimes I would be brought into the middle too, and they would dance to me.

The day when he or she is initiated is a very big day in the life of a Masai;

they are supposed to show no fear nor flinch at the pain. Parents would get very worried about how their sons and daughters would behave. If they behaved badly by showing fear it was a terrible disgrace. The Masai are very emotional people and get easily worked up and sometimes the young men would stand there shaking from head to foot with emotion, especially if the girl concerned happened to be their particular girl friend. They used to invite me to spend the whole night with them while they took part in the ceremonies but as it meant sitting up all night in a smoky hut I never did. The ceremony takes place early in the morning and I would get up and go down to where the people were gathered. I have only been to a girls' initiation and never to a boys', where naturally, being a woman, I would not have been welcome. I would find that the girls had been sitting in a river or dam, in cold water up to their waists until all their nether regions had become numb with the cold; they would then sit down on the ground each leaning against her sponsor. They would open their legs wide and the woman who performed the clitorodectomy would quickly make the cut; it took less than a minute. The girls would sometimes then get up and dance again with the blood running down their legs. They would then be taken off to a hut where they would stay for the next few weeks. I am told that the actual operation is not so painful; the painful time comes the next day or two when you have to walk and especially when you urinate, but normally the cut only takes a few days to heal. The girls would be left for a few days in a hut by themselves, looked after only by the sponsors. They were supposed to be fattened up during this period and had to drink a greal deal of milk. As they were not allowed to wash with water they would rub ashes on their bodies. When they went out during this period they would wear long leather clothes with hoods over their heads. If you happened to meet them, they wouldn't speak or answer your greeting but would clap on their legs with their hands. Occasionally I used to go and visit them in their seclusion and talk to them. They would sing me special songs that were sung at that time. They then had to go through more ceremonies, mainly to do with cleansing, and eventually they would emerge dressed up in their bridal finery with a lot of beads, and were taken off to their husbands.

Most parents would take trouble to arrange a marriage that they thought would be suitable for their daughter. They would try and find a reliable young man and they were very particular about the relationships and what sort of families they came from. They would go into the genealogy carefully. Sometimes, however, girls were married off to old men who had other wives. This was usually when they had not behaved themselves well during their initiation, or if for some other reason they couldn't be married to a young man. I suppose all this business of initiation gave them confidence and made them self-reliant, which was very much what my season in London had been meant to do for me.

The boys had to undergo a series of frightening ordeals. Many of these are secret, but the general idea of all of them was that they had to show that they had courage and resolution to face a frightening situation. The Masai are trained from early childhood to stand pain and show courage. They start as small children by piercing their ears. They make small holes in their ears with a match stick stuck through; each day or two they have to take out whatever was there before and replace it with something bigger. Their ears can become quite enormous – they could easily hold a jam pot by the time they have finished – and hang down in loops; they hang all kinds of earrings in them. Children have their two centre bottom milk teeth knocked out and as soon as they get their second teeth, they are dug out with a knife. They also burn marks on their arms and legs – they use a special kind of leaf for this which they roll up into a funnel, set on fire and then place on their arms and legs until it burns and leaves a scar. They are supposed to hold the burning leaf against their skin for as long as it takes them to run round one of their huts. You will notice on most Masai and the Kalenjin (which includes the Tugen and Nandi) people rows of scars on their thighs and forearms. It is not only a matter of bearing pain; they think these marks look beautiful on their bodies.

The boys during their time of seclusion go round with bows and arrows. The arrows are blunt and they have no head on them, just a thick end. They shoot birds with these and hang them round their houses in the bush. The Uasin Gishu Masai perform an initiation on similar lines to the Nandi people which is rather different from the other Masai. I used to go and visit the boys in their hut, which they call *emenjit*, and they would sing me songs. (Women aren't really supposed to go to this hut but I was exempt from the rule.) They have a special song that they sing in the early morning and in the evening, called *engataet*. Unfortunately I could never understand all the words as I didn't know the Masai language well enough. When the boys come out of their seclusion they are dressed in women's clothes for a day or two and walk about in these. Their heads are shaved and they are then considered warriors. After this they let their hair grow long – it is only the warriors who are permitted to have long hair. When they reach the stage of becoming elders, their hair is once again shaved.

Deloraine was in a traditional Masai area but had been included in the area for European settlers when the agreement was made with the Masai in 1911. There was nobody living on the land when my father went there. But some of the elder Masai would show me places on the farm where people had lived and they would tell me that there was a man they called Daktari who had shot a lioness with white paws near the Molo river. I think this must have been Dr Atkinson who came out with Lord Delamere. They would also talk about Martini. He was a Maltese who had come out with Joseph Thomson in 1884 and later became a district officer at Ravine. Some of the very old men said they could remember the Swahili safaris going through Ravine. These were expeditions from the coast, for trade of all kinds, often for slaves and often led by Arabs. They said people were left with broken legs or illnesses to die by the side of the road. They said sometimes you would come across them, and hear them crying for help.

Further down the Molo river there are some caves and opposite the caves had been a large Masai *manyatta*. I was told that the Kikuyu used to come down and trade there. They would bring red earth (*sereka*), beads, tobacco and other things and the Masai would exchange them for goats. They told me that they used to select very thin old goats and make them drink a lot of water to fill them out and make them look fat and then they would trade them with the Kikuyu. The Kikuyu would take them back to where they were camping and during the night the Masai would come and steal them back again. This was the Masai story. I asked them why, if there was a big *manyatta* there, the Kikuyu didn't come and stay in the *manyatta*. The old Masai who was telling me this looked at me in horror and said: 'What, Kikuyu? You couldn't have them there because they stink.'

There had once been a big battle in Menengai Crater between the Laikipiak section of the Masai and the Purko section. The Laikipiak had been vanquished and scattered to the four winds. Even today you find remnants of the Laikipiak in strange places. I have been told that there are some who live not far from Lamu on the coast. They have become Moslemized but I am told they still speak Masai, though I have never met one myself. Even now Masai won't go into the Crater; they consider it haunted. They said that if you put down your *rungu* (club) and look the other way somebody will take it. And at night you can hear the lowing of the ghostly cattle and see the smoke of the fires. The smoke they see is really steam jets coming out of the crater. Menengai is a corruption of Ol Menenga meaning 'the hill of spirits'.

The Masai used to tell me a story about the old days which they thought a great joke. There was a European called 'Nderu' which means 'beard'. He used to do transport with ox-wagons, as quite a few Europeans did in the early days. He used to drive his ox-wagons thorugh the area known as Visoi where there was a big *manyatta* full of Masai warriors. They objected to his passing through their area without paying anything, but he refused to pay. One day they seized him and took off all his clothes and covered him with *sereka* and then told him he could go home like that.

4
The Kikuyu and Luo

Our Kikuyu squatters had come to the farm in the early 1920s when my father first went there. They came from Kiambu. It is traditional with the Kikuyu to settle on other people's land and cultivate it. When the Kikuyu heard that Europeans were buying up large areas of empty land, they thought this was a wonderful opportunity; and they moved with all their sheep and goats onto these farms and became resident labour or squatters. They expected to become rich because at first they were often allowed to cultivate large areas and keep unlimited sheep and goats. As I have explained, they had to work six tickets for the Europeans and they received a wage for this. But this seemed to them well worth doing when they could occupy so much land where they had never been before.

I once asked an old man why he had come and he told me that he had been bewitched by somebody in the Kiambu area and he had in fact died. Now the Kikuyu, when their people were about to die, took them out of the house and put them on the edge of the forest so that they would not pollute the house by dying in it. In theory, someone would sit by them until they did actually die, and then they would leave them to be eaten by the hyenas. They never buried their people. This old man told me that this is what had happened to him; he had died and had been left there for several days. The maggots had even started to devour his flesh, when miraculously he came back to life again. When he had regained his strength, he decided not to stay in that area any more. He didn't want to be bewitched and die again, so he came to us.

I think there were many stories like this behind the moves. Some of them however came simply because they had no land of their own. The squatters at first were under very few restrictions as to where they could cultivate and how much stock they could keep but gradually as the Europeans developed their farms they could not afford to have people all over the place and so imposed more and more restrictions. One of my first tasks when I started running the farm was to sort out the squatters. At that time we had no fenced boundaries and some of our squatters were living on neighbours' land and some of my neighbours' were living on ours; I had to get them all put into the right areas and settle how much they might cultivate.

When I was a small child the Kikuyu used to come and dance in the garden in front of our house on special days like Christmas and they used to cover themselves with oil and wear skins and beads and bells on their legs. But by the 1930s they had come under the influence of the missionaries who had told them that dancing was indecent and immoral and so they had given it up. They too had initiation ceremonies and circumcised both boys and girls as the Masai did, but they were very secretive about it and they never used to invite me to their celebrations. This was partly because there had been great agitation against female circumcision by the missionaries, who thought it was a useless operation and could only cause trouble later when the girls gave birth. It became quite a political issue; indeed in 1929 it became the first big issue raised by a young mission-educated Kikuyu called Johnston Kamau, better known later as Jomo Kenyatta. The missionaries refused to baptize people who circumcised their daughters. It is true that the circumcision operation for the girls could cause scar tissue which might make childbirth difficult but judging by the number of babies that are born from women who are circumcised I don't think the proportion can be very high. There was also the idea that it prevented women from getting their full pleasure from sex and so it would make wives more faithful to their husbands. But again, judging by what goes on nowadays, I do not think this can be very effective. The Kikuyu still circumcise their girls, not all of them, but the majority. At Deloraine, at the beginning of the Christmas holidays, I am usually asked to supply my Land-Rover and driver to take the boys and girls away, the boys to hospital where they are circumcised, the girls to a special woman who operates on them. Then they all come back to Deloraine. In about a week or two they have healed up and and are walking about in coloured sheets as a sign that they are going through initiation. I have asked several women why they still circumcise their daughters and they say it is because they keep pestering them to be done. The girls are probably only eleven or twelve and really have no idea what they were going to do to themselves. Nowadays the operation for girls has been banned by the President.

The Luo were people who came up the Nile many years ago and settled on the south-eastern side of Lake Victoria. They are agriculturalists but they also keep cattle. They are Nilotics and speak a language of quite a different family from the Kikuyu. Many of them came to work on the European farms as casual labour, especially on the tea estates and sisal plantations. They were engaged for only short periods at a time and then they would go back to their home areas. Those we had on the farm stayed for many years but even so they were still known as casual labourers. Our Luo did most of the heavy work. The ox drivers were usually Luo and they also used to work in the maize fields, carting and humping sacks of maize. They were very strong and like all the Nilotic people who came from a hot country, they had traditionally always gone next to naked and wore virtually no clothes, only beads. They were uncircumcised and the circumcised tribes were rather contemptuous of them. They used to knock out six of their bottom teeth, so they had a big space in their lower jaw. They were usually jolly, friendly people. When not working they had a habit of strutting about with their hands folded across their chests and they used to smoke long pipes. The men used to wrestle, and were very fond of football – we had a football team known as the DTs (Deloraine Team). They only danced very occasionally, and when they did, their dances were not very interesting; they would just circle around in a sort of jog trot holding up clubs and then one of them would rush out as if he was about to attack someone and shake the club and shout and then go back again. This was really in friendship but for anybody who wasn't used to it, it might be rather frightening. The women used to form a circle in a crouching attitude and waggle their bottoms about.

They had a type of harp that they played, called a *nyatiti*, I recall a man who smoked *bhang* (cannabis) and must have gone mad. He started playing all night as well as all day. He hardly stopped for a moment, even to have any food. Then people told me that he was threatening to come up to the house and kill me. I thought this very strange but did nothing. Eventually he appeared and he started playing on my verandah. He wouldn't stop but didn't seem aggressive; it was obvious he had gone out of his mind. However, after a few hours he stopped to get food and drink and we took the opportunity to seize his harp and hid it right at the far end of the cellar beneath the house. When he came back and asked for his harp, we told him where it was and when he went down to get it locked the door on him. We then called the police. In the end I gave some money to two Luo and told them to take him home, and I never saw him again.

Sometimes people worked so long in the European areas that they couldn't remember where they originally came from. There was an old man called Maresa who came from somewhere on the Ugandan border. He said he did remember his home but he had left it when he was a young boy, I think before the First World War, and he had been in the European areas ever since. Half a century later, when he was very old, he had no wife or children to look after him. He still did his own cooking and fetched his own water but I wondered what would become of him when he couldn't. He didn't work, just hung around and did odd jobs for other people. He wasn't employed by me, so he wasn't earning wages. He was too old to work properly, but I gave him a job in the garden cutting down long grass and the money he earned I put in a post office savings account for him; I gave him no cash. After some time when he had saved a few hundred shillings, as he had only rags I bought him some decent clothes – long trousers, a shirt, a jacket and a hat. He was very pleased and looked quite smart. He still had some money left and I asked if he would like to go home. He said he would, and yes, his family would be pleased to see him. I found out from the police in Rongai that they had to escort someone back to the area where he came from and the police inspector kindly said that the old man could go with them. I was most relieved as I felt sure he would get lost if he went on the train by himself. So off he went and that was the last I saw of him. I thought that he must be living happily with his family, but two or three years later I heard to my sorrow that when he reached home the young men there had set on him. They thought that as he had been working for Europeans all these years, he must have saved up a lot of money; when he said he had none, they knocked him down and he died.

When I first started running the farm in the early 1930s, the Kikuyu were beginning to get interested in education and they asked if they could start a school and if I would find a teacher. They built a mud and wattle building with a thatched roof and made some benches. The children just had slates on which to write; they had no proper desks. I managed to find a teacher; he was paid the comparatively high wage of twenty shillings a month. I wrote to the Scotch Mission in Kikuyu to get him. Unfortunately, after a short while people complained to me that he had seduced one of his pupils and I had rather an embarrassing correspondence with the Mission.

Very few Luo brought their children to the farm, although some of them did have their wives with them. So there were no Luo children who wanted to go to school. The Masai flatly refused to send anybody to school. They said they preferred their own way of life and didn't want to learn European ways. So virtually all the children who attended the school were Kikuyu. Over the years our school grew larger, class by class, and other people started sending their children until we got a grant from the Education Department and eventually reached seven standards. Nowadays there are over 300 children in the school. They take an exam at the end of their eighth year and those who are lucky go on to secondary school. These are very few, probably only three or four every year. However, some of the children who started in this humble way have done well in the world. One boy is now an architect; he went to a university in Denmark to qualify and now has his own practice. Several girls are qualified nurses; one is a journalist. Another boy is manager of one of the garages in Nakuru and many others have quite good jobs in Government offices. Often I am greeted by people in Nakuru whom I don't recognize and I find that they used to be at the Deloraine School. There is one Masai who is now a senior civil servant with degrees from both Britain and America who tells me, although I don't remember the incident, that I once caught him sucking the milk from one of our cows. I scolded him for this and told the relative with whom he was staying that he should be sending the boy to school, instead of allowing him to run round wasting his time. Apparently my advice was taken.

I was much struck by differences of character, even within one family. You will find families where there are hard-working boys and girls who get on and get into a university, but in the same family one or two brought up in the same conditions who are perfectly useless – they will not work, they refuse to attend school; they just play around and when they grow up they can get no decent jobs. Some even end up in jail. They had the same chances as their brothers and sisters but they just hadn't got the will to work hard and to get on in the world.

It is sad that girls are sometimes seduced when they are still in primary school. When that happens the girl is expelled and in due course she has a baby. Sometimes the man marries her but more often he is just another schoolboy who has no means of getting married and the girl is left with a baby and no one to support her. Of course no one will marry her and so there is nothing left for such a girl but prostitution, which means more babies. I counted not long ago twelve unmarried girls on the farm with forty-nine children between them. This is one reason why the Masai didn't like sending their girls to school. They said they would either fail and become prostitutes or succeed and think themselves better than their husbands.

5
The Forest

Londiani, the volcanic mountain behind Deloraine, is covered with forest, all the highest parts thick bamboo. When you walk in the forest, it is like going into another world. It is dark, deep and mysterious; beneath your feet the ground is damp with leaf mould; the sunlight filters through the trees; you can hear all kinds of strange noises and smell all kinds of strange smells. There are still many wild animals here including rhino, bongos and a herd of buffalo, as well as giant forest hog, bush pig and several kinds of small antelope – duikers, sunnis and bushbuck, even the odd waterbuck. There are colobus monkeys, blue monkeys, baboons and many small mammals like hyraxes and squirrels. There is a wide variety of birds, including turacoes, trogans, hornbills and even crested eagles.

Traditionally, the people who lived in the forest were called Wa Ndorobo. They keep no stock; they live entirely by hunting and gathering honey and berries. They eat monkeys, hyraxes and any other animals that they can trap or shoot with their bows and arrows. The story of the Wa Ndorobo, who call themselves 'Okiek', is that when God was making the world and giving out the cattle, he had a huge cow hide which came down from heaven to earth and all the cattle walked down this hide and were distributed at the bottom. The first Ndorobo came along and cut the hide so that the cattle couldn't walk down it any more. God was angry and said that because of this the Wa Ndorobo should never have any cattle. They used to say they hated milk and that it was disgusting to drink it.

Nobody knows who exactly the Wa Ndorobo are – whether they are descendants of the original pygmy inhabitants, who were here before the other Africans came, or whether they are people who lost their cattle and were compelled to take refuge in the forests. They are probably a mixture of the two. The Kikuyu talk about people called 'Athi', who were in the forest before themselves; they say they bought their land from these Athi. They also talk of some people called the Ngumba, who were very small with enormous heads, which caused them to overbalance and fall. They couldn't get up again without help, so they used to carry whistles in order to summon their friends to help them when they fell. If there is any truth in this, it may be a memory of the ancestors of the Wa Ndorobo.

The Wa Ndorobo are usually small and light-coloured, with rather pointed faces and bright beady eyes. They are very quick and intelligent. They were the only people in Kenya who were not allotted a reserve of their own by the Colonial Government. Sometimes they used to visit my father and ask him if he could do anything to help them. The Forest Department and others have cut down much of the indigenous forest in order to plant conifers and this means that the Wa Ndorobo have lost their traditional habitat. In the old days the forest would be divided up amongst the Wa Ndorobo families, each getting their bit. Nobody else was allowed to hunt there and any honey or animals there belonged to that family.

There was an Ndorobo called Arap Less who lived in the forest behind Deloraine. He had been born there and his father had lived there before him. There was nothing he didn't know about the forest; he knew every tree by name and he could tell you the uses of all the various plants, what medicines could be made out of them, what you could do with the different barks and wood. He was from the 1910 circumcision group, which is called *nyonge*, and must have been more than ninety when he died – a remarkable age by African standards. To the end he still got around very well and his eyesight was unimpaired. It is a pity that all his forest lore is not recorded because this knowledge will die with him, though I have tape-recorded long conversations with him. His sons know nothing about the forest; they all work in towns. He was an expert tracker and made beautiful bows and arrows. His house was like an armoury, with all kinds of traditional weapons lying about or tucked into the thatch. He used to try to teach me something about tracking and the habits of animals and the uses of plants. In his younger days we gave him a rifle and he shot buffalo and other animals that came down and damaged our crops. He spoke Masai, Kalenjin and Kiswahili. I don't think there is an actual Okiek language; if there is, it is a dialect of Kalenjin or Masai. What they speak depends, I think, on the area in which they live.

Arap Less used to tell me stories. He told of a creature called *enkokopi* who lived in the forest, who was half stone, half flesh, with one eye and one leg, and who cried like a man. He also told me about an old lady who went into the forest to collect firewood. It started to rain and she took shelter under a large tree. Then to her horror she saw the tree trunk move and realized that it was not a tree at all but an elephant's leg! Another story he told was about two young Masai who one day captured an Ndorobo and told him they would kill him. He did not think there was much chance of escape, so he begged them to kill him quickly. He asked them to make their swords very sharp and – to make sure that they killed him at once – to stand on either side of him and both strike together so as to cut off his head. The Masai agreed to this and they both struck. The Ndorobo ducked – and the Masai cut off each other's heads.

I used to enjoy walking in the forest with Arap Less – but it wasn't exactly walking as I had to bend almost double most of the way because I was bigger. He went at a brisk jog-trot and it was exhausting trying to follow and keep up. He used to ask me sometimes: 'What will you do if we meet a rhino?' I would tell him I should have to climb a tree. He would laugh at me and ask how I could climb a tree with shoes on. He would climb any tree, even a completely straight tree trunk with no branches, and he would be up it like lightning. He would frequently disappear up trees to look for honey as we went along. There is a little bird called the honey guide which comes and chitters at you when it wants you to follow it; if you do, it will take you to where there is honey and then of course you must give it some for itself. Arap Less would show me tracks and tell me what animals had made them and what they were doing, where they had laid down, where they had stopped. He would show me their dung and tell me what plants they had been eating. Some of the trees would be covered with mud where big animals such as the rhino had rubbed themselves after wallowing.

The sides of the crater are very steep and the top of the mountain is nearly 10,000 feet high; you would find completely different wild flowers and plants there from on the farm. Arap Less would sometimes dig out some roots or cut branches off a plant and he would tell me that he was going to make it into some kind of medicine. I remember once he said he must collect something which he called 'cold medicine'. After he had dug it out he brought it to show me and it smelt very strongly of menthol. I don't know what it was really. Some of the most common trees that grow in the forest are known as *karakira*; it is a kind of witch-hazel and when in flower has a very strong medicinal smell.

There are strange noises in the forest. The bamboo cracks and makes a loud bang and if you weren't used to it, you might think it was some large animal about to burst through the undergrowth. The trees rub against each other and make creaking sounds. All the same, I always had a feeling of tranquillity when I was walking in the forest or sitting under a tree waiting while Arap Less went off on one of his excursions. It is sad that so much of the indigenous forest in Kenya has been cut down, either for cultivation or for planting conifers. A lot of the trees had little commercial value, though some of the cedar or juniper (as they really are), are used for fence posts and there is some *podo* which makes good timber, as well as olive and several other sorts of trees which can make building material. It has been Government policy to lease sections of this forest to the Forest Department employees for a fixed period. Their first step is to chop down and remove any valuable cedar. Then the charcoal burners come. Charcoal can only be made from certain types of trees; when all these have been burned, the lessees cut down and burn any remaining trees on the spot. Then they cultivate the land and plant maize, beans and potatoes, which they grow for about two or three years. Then they plant the young conifer seedlings. These have been grown in a nursery and are about one year old. They are planted out nine feet by nine and the Forest Department workers continue to plant their food crops amongst them and in this way the trees are looked after and kept cultivated without expense. After a period of about five years, depending on the area and the type of tree, they are too big for crops to grow beneath them; they form a canopy, shutting out the sun. They are then left to mature by themselves. The sad part about planting conifers is that the area becomes quite sterile as far as any other plants are concerned. There is then no food available for animals or birds, so they all have to move off elsewhere. The timber of course is useful and valuable, especially now as there is a paper mill in Kenya. On Mount Londiani there is still about nine thousand hectares of forest that hasn't been touched, mainly in the crater, and I hope that this will be preserved for ever, especially as it is an important water catchment area. The President has now issued a decree that no more indigenous forest is to be cut.

PART IV

On the Job

1
Time Off in Kenya

It was in 1934 that I began to manage the farm and for the next forty-five years it was never far from my thoughts. In a way I was always learning and always on the job; like anyone else, however, I did sometimes take time off.

My mother died in 1938 and was not well during the last years. My father was more and more wrapped up in politics and had to be a great deal in Nairobi, and Moy was often away too; so I was very much on my own. But though my father left the farm entirely to me, he still took an interest in what I did. He always said he didn't mind where I went by day or night in my car but he made one stipulation. I must always take at least one African with me who was supposed to help me put on chains or push me out of the mud if we got stuck, or run with a message if the car broke down. Sometimes when we were travelling at night we used to get lost and end up in an African village, where we had to stop and ask the way. Often the people used to rush away screaming with fright. The African with me explained that they thought we were coming with tin cans to seize people and take blood out of their veins to make some sort of medicine. My car was a dilapidated old thing and they must have thought the rattles were blood containers in the back.

There were other advantages in always having Africans in the car with me. They used to tell me the names of plants, trees, hills and rivers as we drove along and they would point out the different people and tell me what tribe they belonged to. I learned to differentiate between the tribes by their clothing and markings. I learned to recognize the beadwork on a woman's earrings and tell whether she was a Masai or Kalenjin; to know that a woman with an unshaved head covered in red mud had a child undergoing initiation, or that a child with a long tuft of hair on the front of his head had an elder brother or sister recently dead. Sometimes we would be travelling for hours and we would discuss life as we went along.

There was one cinema in Nakuru and sometimes a few friends would meet to see a film; afterwards we would have a moonlight picnic on the edge of Menengai Crater. We cooked bacon and eggs and sang songs. In those days there were no tape recorders or transistor radios and none of us had much talent for music but we would laugh at our own efforts and enjoy ourselves. Menengai lived up to its reputation with the Africans when a young European murdered his girl friend up there. Another girl had been killed a few years before; and two people committed suicide by driving their cars over the escarpment. But we didn't think of that.

We would occasionally picnic, too, along the shores of Lake Nakuru. By the end of the 1930s this lake was almost dry. Only a small pool of water was left in the middle, and in dry weather there was a huge expanse of soda dust, which used to blow over Nakuru town and give people sore eyes and throats. There was even talk of grassing over the whole area. Once one of my friends took me there in his car during a dance in the Nakuru Club and started to drive at full speed across this level stretch. Unluckily we went full tilt into a wet patch and stuck. This was awkward as we were supposed to be at the dance, and if we had been caught we should have suffered endless teasing. Lake Nakuru was about three or four miles from the town, so all we could do was for my friend to walk back there and call for help, leaving me alone in the car. After much pushing and heaving and cutting of branches to put under the wheels we finally managed to get out and went back to the dance.

On Saturdays we would often have dances, perhaps in a club. There would be an amateur band and we would dance till early morning. There were always numerous Africans looking through the windows. I suppose they liked to see how the *wazungu* were disporting themselves. And then there was a long drive back home to Deloraine or to where you were staying for the night. Sometimes if it was wet and muddy we would have to get out and push or put chains on the wheels. This was tiresome in a long evening dress, which had to be hitched up and tied round one's waist.

At New Year and in July there were race weeks in Nairobi. There would be racing and polo tournaments and dances and people would come from all over the country. I always enjoyed the racing – though polo never appealed to me – and the few days away from the farm made a pleasant break. All the same I was rather put out when people greeted me, dressed up in my best, with: 'How are the cows?' I felt as if I had dung in my hair! At that time the kind of man I admired was one who could break a horse, calve a cow or overhaul a tractor, so most of my dancing partners were farm managers. Many of them were not very good dancers. As we trudged around the hot and stuffy room, often to a rather indifferent amateur band, my mind would wander to Masai dances that I had been to, out in the open, under the stars with the people leaping up and down to a slow chant. I sometimes wished I was there instead.

When there was a polo tournament or race meeting and a dance near Deloraine we usually had a party in the house and I would invite some young men to stay. Loder did not always approve. I remember once she fixed one of these young men with her beady eye and asked: 'Don't you never do no work?' He was a hard-working farm manager but he said to her: 'Well you see, Loder, polo *is* my work.' She sniffed and went off muttering to herself. Another time when the house was already rather full of visitors I told Loder that she could make up beds for two young men in a room adjoining my bedroom with a connecting door. 'What?' she exclaimed. 'Them polo players! I'll get the key and lock the door.' She did, and took the key away.

My chief recreation was my horses and what I enjoyed best was hunting at Molo. The hunt took place on Sunday mornings and I would send my horse on overnight with a syce and it would sleep in the stables of a friend near the meet. I would go early in the morning or on Saturday evening. It was a complete change from Deloraine. Most of the farms where the meets were held were two or three thousand feet higher than us, some over nine thousand feet above sea level. It was cold at night, even frosty. Daffodils and primroses grew in the gardens. Most of the houses were made of cedar with shingle roofs, and very attractive. On Sunday morning we would get up in time for the meet at eight. The hounds were foxhounds imported from various packs in England; the huntsman was European and the whips were Africans. It was amusing to hear them calling the hounds in the right tone of voice and using the expressions that whips use in England. We hunted reedbuck; we used to draw the big swamps and usually had a good run. I am very fond of animals and have spent many hours cherishing small buck that have been brought to me to rear; I would have been very distressed if anyone had killed them. But for some reason hunting gave me great pleasure. Maybe it is because hunting is a basic human instinct. It was lovely galloping over the hills in Molo. At that time there were very few fences and the hills were covered in red oat grass. To feel a fit horse under you galloping over the springy turf gave you a wonderful sensation and to watch hounds working and hear them giving tongue is always a keen pleasure. It would take my mind off farm worries as nothing else did.

We also had gymkhana race meetings and I enjoyed riding in these. My little mare Islette, Paulette's daughter, turned out a good racehorse and I won a number of races on her. She could stay forever. These were all flat races. I usually rode in the ladies' races but sometimes I would ride in the men's as well.

For holidays we went to the coast and rented a little coast house called a *banda*. These were made of coral blocks, very open, with *mukuti* (palm leaf) roofs, and they were usually built along the beach front. In those days there were very few people on the beaches and you could walk for miles without seeing anyone. Occasionally we went for moonlight walks along the beach and would plunge into the sea, often without bathing suits, all girls together. If there were men in the party, they would do the same on another part of the beach.

Once I was staying with the Sladens in a house they had rented at Nyali near Mombasa. Ruth and I decided to walk to Bamburi, which is about three miles along the beach. We met a few fishermen mending their nets and preparing their boats and exchanged greetings. In their usual friendly way they asked where we were going and where we had come from and we told them. As we went on further, we met a man by himself who asked where we were going and whether we would be coming back the same way. We told him and thought no more about it. On the way back Ruth was walking in front of me; it was very low tide and we walked most of the way on the sand as the coral was very sharp. As we rounded a point, the same man was sitting there; as we passed he suddenly sprang up, ran past me, seized hold of Ruth, knocked her down and sat on her. We were only wearing rubber shoes, and had nothing we could use as a weapon. All I could do was jump on top of him, put my hands round his neck and press my thumbs into his eyeballs. But he was very strong and he shook me off. We were both screaming blue murder and he was swearing at us very volubly with English swear words. I remembered the fishermen round the next point but they couldn't see us from where they were working. I jumped up and ran till they could see me and yelled frantically for them to come and help. They came at once and the attacker ran off. The fishermen said that they knew him and he was mad. We were naturally both rather frightened and we asked them to come with us as far as home. It was about three miles and all the way we saw the man trailing us above on the cliff. When we got home we reported what had happened to the police. They asked us to walk there the next day and they would be behind us disguised as fishermen. I had been wearing shorts which I wasn't accustomed to and my legs had been terribly sunburnt and sore so next day Mrs Sladen took my place. The same man did come and they caught him. We found later that he had recently been released from a lunatic asylum in Nairobi; I suppose that is where he had learnt his flow of English swear words.

I used to stay with various friends from time to time. One of the places I enjoyed most was Kapsiliat at Moi Ben, which is west of the Rift Valley in the foothills of the Cherangani Mountains. In order to get there we had to travel over very high country. Almost on top there is a little lake called Narasha. There is a story that it was made by a giant who fell down: you can see where his arms and legs landed as there are four little valleys each leading out of the lake. We came down from there to the Uasin Gishu Plateau. Most of the farmers there were Afrikaners, who had come up from South Africa. Kapsiliat belonged to my father's friend Mervyn Ridley, whose wife Sybil had made a beautiful garden under the *podo* trees which surround the house. There were great beds of agapanthus, hydrangeas and cinerarias and every kind of shrub and flower.

They had a large lake and a turbine which pumped up plenty of water for the garden. There were trout in the lake and in the Moi Ben river. The land was rather hilly and rough which made it difficult to farm and it was thirty-five miles from the nearest railhead, which put up transport costs. But they had a herd of red poll cattle, and a stud of thoroughbred horses – Mervyn always had a few in training. Sometimes my father's and Mervyn's friend Cecil Hoey would come over; he had a farm nearby and the three would tell each other wonderful stories, some very scurrilous. Cecil had come out very early and had been a hunter before the First World War. Mervyn had also come out before the war and between the three of them they knew almost everything about all the settlers in the country.

Another place I liked to visit was Kilima Kiu. This was a dairy farm about sixty miles out of Nairobi on the Mombasa side, belonging to Frank Joyce and his wife. It had been started before the First World War as an ostrich farm by three young men in partnership. They collected ostriches and their eggs from the plains, tamed the birds and clipped their feathers for sale. Before the war these feathers were the height of fashion but afterwards, when open motor cars became popular, big feather hats were not practical. The partnership broke up and the land was sold. It is very attractive country, open plains with acacia trees and views for miles and miles around. When the Joyces first went there it was almost waterless but they made boreholes and dams. They had a daughter, Anne, who was almost exactly my age. She helped her father on the farm during the war and after he died she continued to run it.

Next door to Kilima Kiu was Wami. This land had been bought by Frank Howden and his wife Peggy just before the Second World War. It was over 20,000 acres but cheap because it was waterless. But by making dams and putting down boreholes they too managed to turn it into a first-class beef and sheep ranch. These were all much bigger farms than Deloraine.

We used to have visitors of all kinds at Deloraine, some over from Britain. In those days they had to come by sea and it took about three weeks on the boat, so they usually stayed a long time. One of our most frequent visitors before her marriage was Alice Scott, the daughter of my Uncle John Buccleuch. She loved being in Kenya. She had her own car and Kikuyu servant and would travel all round the country staying with friends and going on camping safaris. She was a talented painter and watercolourist.

In 1936 she married Prince Henry, Duke of Gloucester, which meant she had to attend endless public functions and have a large wardrobe of clothes, some of which she would very kindly send me after she had worn them a few times. They were beautiful clothes made by such people as Norman Hartnell and as my salary didn't go very far this was a tremendous help to me.

In 1938 she and Prince Henry came out to Kenya together with her brother-in-law, Geoffrey Hawkins, and they took me on a safari with a hunter called Alan Black. He was an eccentric old man who had once been an ivory poacher, so he said. We went first to Isiolo and then went down the Tana river where Prince Henry wanted to shoot a Hunter's hartebeest. Alan Black didn't like women and didn't like having Alice and me in the party. He liked telling tall stories which he said Africans had told him. As I spoke Swahili quite fluently, and Alice spoke a little, we used to tell him, to his considerable irritation, that he was talking nonsense and that the Africans had never said any such thing. He took Prince Henry out shooting most evenings and Alice usually went with him. I was left to go with Geoffrey Hawkins, who one day shot a buffalo, thereby annoying Prince Henry who hadn't even seen a buffalo. I think Alan Black had taken good care that he should never get near any animal that could be remotely dangerous. This was the time of the Munich crisis and at one moment it looked as though they would have to cut short their holiday and go back to Britain. However, they were able to stay and we ended the trip by a night at Treetops, where later the Queen was staying when her father died.

When I could get away from the farm I loved going on camping safaris with my friends. We usually put up only one tent for dressing and slept round the fire on camp beds under the stars. One night, I remember, we found elephant footprints about ten feet away from our beds. They must have walked right past us in the night without our hearing them. We usually had rifles with us to use if necessary and sometimes to shoot for the pot – occasionally one of the party would shoot a lion – but shooting was not the object. We often caught trout in the mountain rivers and we would bathe in the icy water and lie afterwards on the hot rocks to get warm and dry again.

Before the Second World War there used to be a battalion of King's African Rifles stationed at Meru. Sometimes Moy and I would go on safaris with some of the officers. We used to go to what is now Samburu National Park and around Isiolo. I remember going once to see a refugee camp for Ethiopians there, after Ethiopia was invaded by Italy. The Northern Frontier District was a 'closed area' and you had to have a permit from the Provincial Commissioner to enter it. He would never give us one to go to Wajir, as he said that the soldiers might be suddenly called out to quell a quarrel amongst the Somalis over a waterhole, and then what could they do with us? We used to laugh at this, and tell him the real reason was that the battalion didn't want us to see the beautiful Somali girls they used to keep.

About 1935 several of us joined the 'FANYs' (First Aid Nursing Yeomanry), of whom a unit had been raised by Lady Sidney Farrar who had a farm at Mau Summit. She had built a camp; the barracks consisted of split bamboo huts with thatched roofs and earth floors. We used to go there every year for training for two weeks. The FANYs were supposed to drive vehicles and give the wounded first aid, so our training consisted of learning very elementary mechanics and some first aid. The camp was run on supposedly military lines. We were only about twenty girls. The latrine had eight seats in a row without any divisions so we all had to sit there in full view of each other. At mealtimes we were only allowed one plate for two courses; when we demurred we were told that was the way it was done in the Army. We also had to do drill. We were terribly bad at it, always going in the wrong direction and colliding with each other. I couldn't take this very seriously and used to start giggling, so I was put on a charge for 'laughing on parade'. My punishment was to be given a bar of iron about the size of a bar of soap and a hacksaw and told to saw through it.

I had taken up some ponies to ride in my spare time as there was a polo ground nearby with some stables. On the first evening I heard bugles blowing but paid no attention and carried on feeding my horses and bedding them down. In due course I went back to camp and found that I was in terrible trouble as I should have been back before the bugle blew.

Again I was put on a charge. This time my punishment was to run up and down the parade ground with a rifle held over my head. Worse still, one day I was mess orderly, which meant I had to lay the tables for the meals, light the fires and do odd jobs like that. Bissie Dudgeon, with whom I shared a hut, was also an orderly. We were busy with our work one evening when some of our boy friends who were working on nearby farms came to visit us. Finding us busy, they went to our hut and sat on our beds waiting for us to come. They were discovered there by a sergeant and there was a terrible to-do: we were going to be court-martialled because we were entertaining men in our bedroom. The next day we were taken to the orderly room and given a long dressing down and told we were the scum of the army. But there was a shooting match that afternoon between the Kenya Defence Force, which was the men's territorial regiment, and the FANYs and Bissie Dudgeon and I were both in the team. We won the competition – and heard no more of the court-martial. We used to have this competition every year and usually won, though the .303 army rifles were rather heavy and used to give us black and blue shoulders. One year I also won the revolver competition, shooting with a Colt army revolver.

An old man called Major Drought, who lived near our camp, used to come and lecture us. His theme was what ghastly things would happen to girls if there were a native rising. He said we would be tied up by our ankles head down over a fire and slowly roasted. He also told us we would be issued with cyanide pills which would be sewn into the collars of our uniforms and we should be able to bite them out and do ourselves in before we suffered a fate worse than death. Most of us had been brought up in Kenya and used to treat him as a joke but one girl who was more of a newcomer to the country fainted and had to be carried from the room.

Once we had a church parade. I was the right-hand man (or woman) in the front rank and I was told that to keep a straight line I must look at a certain fence post and never take my eyes off it. This I did, and fell up to my waist into a large antbear hole that lay in our path. Everyone behind trampled over me.

These camps were great fun but it was difficult to take them seriously. However the FANYs did a good job when the war came.

2

Firm Beliefs

My father was Elected Member of the Legislative Council for the Rift Valley and also the Leader of the European Elected Members after Lord Delamere's death in 1931; he was also on numerous other boards and committees. That was why I had to look after the farm. He believed that the white and black people were complementary to each other; each needed the other to develop the country. He thought it essential that the Europeans should be 'of the best type'; they should have some education so that they could set an example to the Africans and be their leaders. I think he pictured the Africans eventually abandoning their own culture and taking up the European way of life, which he thought was the best anyone could have. I don't think he ever understood that the Africans might want to do things their own way. Nor did he see that as Africans became more educated they would want to take up highly paid jobs and positions of responsibility and that the Europeans would resent their competition.

My father always disliked hearing people spoken of as 'pro-native' or 'pro-European'. He said he was neither, he was 'pro-Kenyan'; he firmly believed that what was good for one was good for the other. He had no doubt, either, that Europeans who had lived in Kenya and wanted their children and grandchildren to follow them could rule the country far better than people appointed by the Colonial Office in London, to whom it was 'only a career' and who had no personal stake in the country. Looking back on his views I see now that he was far too idealistic. He put too high a value on the way of life that had evolved in Europe and he expected all Europeans to be unselfish leaders. For some years he represented so-called Arab interests in the Legislative Council. He also knew the Asian members of the Legislative Council quite well and was very friendly with Sir Ali Bin Salim who was the Sultan of Zanzibar's representative as *liwali* on the coast. When we stayed on the coast, it was often at his house at Likoni. But he probably never had a serious political discussion with any African. He couldn't speak Kiswahili well enough to discuss things with any of our local Africans on the farm and I doubt whether he had any contacts with the more educated Africans that he might have found in Nairobi. This was not because he wanted to keep apart, but because there was then such a wide social gap between the races that he really never had the opportunity. If he had been able to talk to Jomo Kenyatta or Harry Thuku or other leading Africans of the time, he would have had a better idea of nationalist feelings. He would have understood African resentment at European dominance and at some of the laws then in force. He might have seen how they felt about segregation in schools and hospitals and especially the restrictions on land tenure. He put such people down as paid agitators in the hands of socialists overseas; he did not think they represented their people. He was firmly convinced that the Europeans had taken no land from the Africans. There had been endless commissions on this, he said, and they had proved that, with the possible exception of very small areas around Kiambu, no land in African occupation had been taken by settlers. But of course he didn't understand the African attitude to land. It wasn't at all the same as in Europe where a person had a piece of land to which he had title and could call his own and no one else could lay claim to it. Africans had no idea of buying and selling land. They were always moving from one place to another. But certain areas were 'theirs', not to sell but to roam over. He sometimes said he regretted the allocation of land in Kenya, some to native reserves and some to settlers. He thought it might have been better to have everybody mixed up, as in Tanganyika; in that way the Europeans would demonstrate to the Africans their superior farming methods and in due course the Africans would copy their systems. He had no doubt that the reason why native reserves were formed was to protect the Africans and stop the Europeans from taking all the best land.

Many people used to come and see him. They came to tell him their problems and to see if he could help them in any way. Some of them had genuine problems, but many others came only to tell him about some strange ideas of their own. Kenya was full of eccentrics. I remember one man who thought an area of land should be divided into small blocks, about fifty acres each, and given to 'European sons of the soil', men of peasant upbringing, who were used to digging their own land and who would employ no paid labour. They would keep cows, bees and poultry and they would live by the sweat of their brow. For every fifty men, fifty girls should be brought out and they would make the butter, cook the food and each marry one of the men. This was the firm belief *he* held. Another one claimed he could increase the acreage of his land by digging depressions and heaping up the soil so that his entire land was a series of mounds. By this he thought he could double his acreage.

My father would get bored with these people and show it and it was sometimes embarassing. I often sat on the verandah listening and he would nod off and give the odd snore or pick up a newspaper and start reading whilst they were still talking. Then there was Elspeth Huxley's father, Jos Grant, who used to write plays; he would come and read them to my father and he would fall asleep. There was also a man who thought the world was coming to an end on a certain day, and he would tell his servants that they need not cook any food. He would sit down and prepare himself for the end. He would sit there and sit there – and after a time he would become rather hungry, so he would decide that perhaps he had made a mistake and it wasn't the right day after all.

There were also the British Israelites who thought the Pyramids of Egypt had been built to foretell events of 4,000 years later. Other people had a firm belief in quite another kind of pyramid. They thought that black and white should be separated and in each area those who could should get to the top, so that there would be a black pyramid and a white pyramid – but one should not rule the other.

At the back of all this was anxiety about the future of Europeans in Africa. There were those who held that African brains never matured after they reached puberty. There were bright African children, they said, but the adults never became intelligent. Some laid the blame for this on the ordeals Africans had to go through during initiation, while some argued that in the tropical sun all adolescents would mature far too fast. My father took little heed of any of these people.

Most of these wild theories and much of the serious discussion in the Twenties and Thirties was because Europeans in Kenya were afraid of the future and also because they had no idea of what Africans were capable of academically. Very few of them had ever met or even heard of an African who was more than semi-literate. If they could have looked into the future, and seen African scientists and other highly skilled African people, they simply would not have believed it.

There were eleven European Elected Members in my father's time. His Rift Valley Constituency stretched from Londiani to Nanyuki, so there was much ground to cover. My father believed that one should always take the broad view of things, and not look at problems from a parochial angle, which some of his colleagues were inclined to do. This made him impatient and intolerant. He was not a man to accept fools gladly and he could be very outspoken, to say the least. Most of the settlers were individualists too and it was a hard job to keep them all pulling as a team. Then, being on the Executive Council put him in a rather odd position. He was virtually Leader of the Opposition to the Government and yet the Executive Council was more or less the Cabinet: many of the subjects that they discussed were confidential, and he could not divulge them to his constituents or fellow members.

What my father and his friends were trying to do was 'develop the country'. They hoped to make the land as productive as possible and raise the standard of living for everyone. The more far-sighted of them realized that a country where the majority of the people were dissatisfied and unhappy could not be ruled successfully. It is because of the hard work and vision of some of the settlers that Kenya, even now, is in so many ways far in advance of most of the other independent African countries. My father's aim was an unofficial majority in the Legislative Council, not necessarily all Europeans. When he retired he wrote a memorandum which he called a 'Draft Outline of Self-Government in Kenya'. This has been deposited with the Institute of Commonwealth Studies in Russell Square, London. Here are some extracts:

It appears to me that all our troubles, political and developmental, arise from this most unsatisfactory, self-destroying bureaucratic form of government under which we suffer, and which places us entirely at the whims of the bureaucrats . . . If we (the Europeans) are to take the proper part in the future development of East Africa, as we should do, we must have further security for ourselves and our own interests, so that we can apply ourselves whole-heartedly to the real development of Kenya . . . Obviously, if one looks far enough ahead this part of the world cannot always be run along narrow racial lines – as the Africans advance in education and political experience they will inevitably demand a greater share in the administration of the country. It is therefore imperative that the European and African races shall attempt to understand each others' points of view and plan to work in the fullest co-operation for the benefit of the country at large. This can only come about if the fears of both races for their own security are satisfied and cease to exist. For this reason it is essential that the Europeans who have made their homes in this country must have that feeling of security. Once that has been fully established and when the Africans have had sufficient time to obtain their political experience, the two races should be able to combine administratively, free from any racial antagonism for the communal good of their mutual country.

3
The War

When war broke out in 1940 between Italy and Britain, Kenya had only a few African troops with British officers and no artillery. Just north of us in Ethiopia there was a very large Italian army, which had recently occupied that country. Kenya was therefore in the 'front line' and nobody knew if we should be invaded. My father decided to resign his seat in the Legislative Council and go back to the Army, where he became the Assistant Military Secretary in Command Headquarters, Nairobi – succeeding Lord Erroll, who was later murdered. His main job was posting officers to the different units and appointments: as he had a very good knowledge of the people in Kenya this suited him well.

I was exempted from service in the FANYs because farming was a reserved occupation but Moy served until she got married. She had finished her education in Europe in 1936 and had come back to Kenya. She took a secretarial course in Nairobi and then my father took her to England in 1937 where she was presented and did the London Season. After that she trained for the stage at the Webber Douglas School of Dramatic Art. War broke out just before she finished the course and she enlisted in the FANYs in England. She was later transferred to the East Africa Command and she worked in the Cypher Office in Nairobi until 1942 when she married Hugo Tweedie. He was in the Scots Guards but had been seconded to the King's African Rifles and had been in Kenya for some years. When she married him, he was commanding one of the KAR battalions. They had two children, Anna and Gavin. In 1945 Hugo was ordered back to his regiment; he was killed in France in April 1945.

Soon after the outbreak of war most of the European young men were called up. Some had been in the KAR Reserve of Officers and others were in the Kenya Defence Force. They left their farms to be run by wives or elderly neighbours. Germans were interned in camps and their farms were given to the Custodian of Enemy Property to manage, and the same applied to Italians. The South African Army sent some units to Kenya early in the war. Nothing much happened for the first few months, but we had to have a blackout and be on the alert because of the Italians in

Ethiopia. Later, when the Kenya Army had been enlarged, they and the South Africans went north through Somalia to Ethiopia, where they fought the Italians. The Italians did not put up much of a fight – their hearts weren't really in the war – and a great many of them were captured and sent to Kenya as prisoners of war. Many of them were released on parole and worked on the farms in different capacities. Two came to work for us, a mechanic and a mason.

Loder left Deloraine and went to run a convalescent home for airmen in Nairobi, so I had to look after the housekeeping as well as the farm. Two elderly Poles, Marilka and Adam Starzenski, came to live in our guest house. They had a son who was in the Polish Foreign Office. He had been posted to London and there he had met some of my cousins, who had written to us and asked us to be kind to these two old people who had had a terrible time. Their part of Poland had been overrun by the Russians and they had been put in a train which travelled three weeks across Russia until eventually they had arrived in Kazakhstan, north of India, where the train stopped and they were ordered to get out. When they inquired what they were to do, they were told they were free to do anything they wished. They had no money and no means of getting food. Most of them were from towns and knew nothing about country life. Adam and Marilka went to the farmhouse of the manager who was running the local communal farm and managed to get accommodation, sleeping on the floor of his kitchen.

With no means of providing for themselves otherwise, they had to resort to stealing. Marilka made little pockets in her skirt, into which she would put ears of barley when they went out into the fields. They were always very hungry. They had been large landowners and later the peasants from their estate in Poland discovered their whereabouts and sent them food parcels. They lived in Kazakhstan for quite a long time, until the Russians made some pact with the Polish leaders and they were allowed to get into a lorry and drive to the Black Sea. From there they caught a boat which took them to Iran; from Iran they were sent to Kenya. At that time there were a lot of Polish refugees in Kenya.

Moy would come with her family and stay at Deloraine when she couldn't accompany Hugo. We had another friend, Elisabeth Church, from the Borders in Scotland, whose husband was also commanding a battalion of the KAR and she would come and stay as well. She had two small children. Both Elisabeth and Moy used to employ Polish girls to help with the children. These girls had usually suffered in much the same way as Adam and Marilka and most of their families had died. They were often hysterical and would sometimes talk about committing suicide but it never came to anything while they were with us.

We would also have troops to stay for their leave. First we had South African soldiers and then sailors from the British Navy in Mombasa. The sailors were charming people as a rule and very appreciative. Some of them had come out of orphanages or boys' homes and had never been in such a house before. They were very amusing about it. Many of them were fitters in the Fleet Air Arm and they would give me files and tools which one couldn't get in the war and which were very useful for me on the farm. I suppose they had filched them from their workshops. Many of them came repeatedly to stay and we got to know them quite well; they in turn would send their friends. We would get letters saying: 'My friend Bob had a nice time for his leave at your house. I wonder if I could come for my leave?' and so the house was always pretty full. Once, much later, one of these young sailors wanted to write a thank-you letter but had forgotten my address. So he sent his letter to Miss Pamela Scott, c/o The Queen, Buckingham Palace, England, and it reached me. A few of my own friends would come on leave too and sometimes my father would send up an officer in need of rehabilitation.

A few of our African labourers also joined the forces, not exactly from patriotism, more from a desire for adventure. Serving together and living at close quarters inspired a great feeling of camaraderie between the European officers and African troops. Our men were used to living in forests and in the bush, and so, when they had beaten the Italians in Ethiopia, they were sent to Madagascar, where the Vichy French were holding out, and then to Burma.

We soon began to get news of friends who had been killed or wounded or taken prisioner. Amongst them was Eddie Sladen, who was killed in Burma deep in the jungle, leaving behind a wife and two small sons. He was in the East African Scouts and his men carried his body back three days' march to headquarters.

During the war, farming became a little easier financially. It was important that we should grow enough food for all the extra people who were in the country and schemes were started to encourage us. Prices went up and we could claim from the Government when we had a crop failure.

Bissie Dudgeon had married a tea planter at Kericho called Gregor Grant and Ruth Sladen had also married a farmer, Dickie Mason. Emily had become very religious; she had joined the Pentecostal Church and devoted her life to missionary work. She would collect drunks, criminals and prostitutes and try to save them – and in some cases she appeared to do so.

Geraldine had been posted in the FANYs to Dar-es-Salaam and had married Michael Macoun, an officer in the Tanganyika Police Force. Later he became the last European Inspector-General of the Ugandan Police. Jean Dudgeon married a civil engineer in the East African Railways and Harbours. They were posted to Uganda and the Nile steamers came under him. Later I did a very enjoyable trip down the river as far as the Sudan border on one of the paddle steamers. It was rather fun sitting on the deck watching the elephants and other animals coming down to drink from the Nile, and at the little stopping places people would come down to the riverside with their produce. The steamers pushed lighters in front of them with masses of people on board and there they would sit with all their goods and chattels. Most were almost naked.

Sometimes my friends would ask me to look after their animals while they were away in the war. Once I stupidly put somebody's mare in the same paddock as an Ayrshire bull. It was quite a large paddock and I thought they would share it amicably. Unfortunately they both felt thirsty at the same time and both went to drink from the trough. The bull attacked the mare and ripped open her stomach so that her guts were hanging out. There was nothing I could do but shoot her. I was just standing there with the gun in my hand, feeling very miserable and wondering how I could explain my stupidity to the owner, when people came running to say that somebody had fallen into one of our dams and was drowning. I rushed there and found a lot of women standing on the bank of the dam howling and screaming; they pointed out where the man had fallen in and not been seen again. I had to strip off my clothes and dive in to see if I could find him. The dam water was very muddy so I couldn't see much when I went under. I groped about for a while but could find nothing and had to give up. I felt sure the man must be dead by that time. I informed the police who said we were to watch the bank, day and night, until the body rose to the surface. This it did after about a week. As I was determined not to lose it again, I tied a rope round the man's neck and hitched it to a nearby bush. When the policeman came he was very annoyed. He said that as the body had been in the water a long time the flesh would be soft and the rope would make a mark around the man's neck which would suggest that he had been strangled. However, luckily, I heard no more of that. But that day had been one of the worst I can remember on the farm.

The daily business of farming went on much as usual. We had very little food rationing, but it was still quite a job feeding all the people that we had in the house from my rather slender financial resources. We had a man with a rifle who would shoot buck, a Kikuyu of partially Athi origin. (The Athi were the hunting people that the Kikuyu said they bought their land from.) We also used to slaughter the Ayrshire bull calves, and of course we had as much dairy produce as we needed and we bought chickens and eggs from the Africans. We had a vegetable garden which Marilka helped to supervise. Adam used to try to supervise the milking but was happier asking the Masai to demonstrate their dances and songs, so I let him have his way. The Italian prisioners kept the machinery going and did quite a bit of building.

We were rationed for petrol and so used horses as much as possible. Elisabeth Church – who later married Bobo, the Duke of Roxburghe, and when he died, Jocelyn Hambro, the banker – was very good with horses and suggested that we should start a Kenya Horse Society and Pony Club. We formed a committee with my father as President and soon we had several branches of the Pony Club going; I was the Chairman of the Njoro Branch for several years.

Some years before, I had been given a lurcher bitch and when the South African Army were in Kenya one of them gave me a greyhound dog. I bred from these two and we started coursing on horses here and on the plains between Menengai and Nakuru. We had good fun galloping over the plains after steinbok and hares and sometimes reedbuck. Some of the soldiers who were stationed nearby used to come too. But as the land became more developed and fenced the dogs would damage themselves. Greyhounds hunt entirely by sight and move very fast; they would often run into a wire fence or other obstacle. I once saw one run into a tree stump and tear the whole of her front leg off at the shoulder. I had to give them up.

I used to do a fair amount of race riding. As there was no proper racing 'under rules' in the war I used sometimes to ride for other people and had to ride against Africans and professional jockeys. Even in those days of racial segregation, no one thought it odd that I should wear the sweat-soaked colours that an African jockey had just worn when I was riding for the same owner in the next race. I could never ride under ten stone, even with a 2 lb saddle, so it meant that I often rode the top-weight good horses and it was exciting when I managed to win.

I used to stay occasionally with my friends Patience and Edward Windley. He was a District Commissioner and when they were posted in Masai country I went with them on safari. We used to go and see the primary schools, and the small boys in white *shukas* (clothes) would all rush up to us and give us their heads to touch, in the Masai manner. Each boy took a cow to school and his mother to milk it. When we went for walks in the evenings, old men would often come up to the DC and beg him not to make them send their boy to school, as they had no one else to herd the stock. Sometimes when the young men were naughty he would send his *askaris* to arrest them, shave their heads – a terrible punishment for a warrior – and send them off to school. Recently one of our Assistant Ministers told me that that had happened to him, and now he was so grateful, as he would never have got to where he was were it not for that DC.

We once went on safari in a lorry, and amongst many others who came with us was a released prisoner, whom we dropped off at his home as we were passing that way. Everyone had turned out to greet him and he was smothered with kisses by his female relatives. Another evening we went out shooting guinea fowl. Patience and I were trying to drive the birds towards the gun when we put up a rhino. We had a Dalmatian dog with us and the rhino, who obviously had never seen such a spotted thing before, started to chase it. Of course the dog ran towards us for protection – while we ran towards Edward! Fortunately, the rhino soon had enough and went off.

During the war some new neighbours arrived who became great friends. They were Swedes, Hans and Viveka Stjernsward. Viveka was about my age, and we had known each other since childhood. The farm they came to had belonged to other Scandinavians, of whom a strange story was told. Mrs Mohr was descended from a fairy. In Norway it is the custom in summer to send the cattle up into the mountains to graze, with a young herdsman. One young man, who was up there for several weeks, had met a lovely girl and fallen in love with her. No one knew who this girl was, nor where she came from; she would never say. But they married and had a family. Then one day when they were getting old the woman disappeared – as suddenly and mysteriously as she had come. Mrs Mohr was her granddaughter. Her husband drowned while crossing a river on safari and so the farm had been sold to the Stjernswards – who built it up into a big dairy and poultry business.

4
Farming after the War

Soon after the war my father went to England for a holiday and for Moy's second wedding. She married David Smiley, an officer in the Royal Horse Guards (The Blues). He had served in the Special Operations Executive (SOE) during the war and had been parachuted into Albania and later into Siam, where he had carried on guerrilla warfare. They later had two children, Xan and Philip.

While my father was in England he made arrangements to turn Deloraine into a limited company. As he had been lent money by some of his relations from time to time in the past, he arranged that some of them should have shares in the company and that one of them should take a mortgage on the land at a low rate of interest. This mortgage was to cause me a great deal of trouble in the years ahead, because the mortgagee held the title deeds of the farm and therefore I could never raise a loan. I had no other security and, as any farmer knows, it is hard to run and develop a farm without borrowing money on occasion. Well-meaning people would advise me to sell off some of the land to pay off these loans, but they didn't realize that to do so I should have had to sell the good land and we would have been left with an uneconomic unit. I doubt if anyone would have bought the waterless, rocky, steep land at the back of the farm and if they had we should have got very little for it. The other possibility would have been to sell stock but we were already understocked and the cattle were the only source of income. The debts did undoubtedly retard the development of the farm considerably.

My father was never good with money. He had never paid his own bills until he was married; he would send all his accounts to his father's chamberlain. He and his brothers were not supposed to run up bills of over a thousand pounds but I don't think much attention was paid to this. When I started running the farm, I soon learnt that it was no good going to my father for help. If I told him I had a problem, he would say that he had given me a job to do and that I should get on with it. It was no good running to him when I got into difficulties. He would never even look at the farm accounts. I must admit to being rather hurt when I took him the balance sheet one day when the farm first started to pay and he waved it away saying: 'It's no good showing me those things, I never understand them.' Sometimes we were very short of cash and I didn't know what to do. Any bit of money that I managed to save went back into developing the farm and occasionally some relative would die and leave me a little legacy and I would put that also into the farm account. It was written down as a loan from me and I would get a small amount of interest. Once, I remember, I went to get the wages for the labour and the bank refused to cash my cheque. I was in despair and had to go back and make some excuse to the men as to why they weren't going to be paid. Luckily it happened to be my twenty-first birthday and a few days later a cheque arrived from my kind relatives in England, who had passed the hat round to give me a present. So I was able to cash this cheque and pay the wages. I did mention once or twice to my father I was putting my own money into the company and all he said was: 'Oh, you shouldn't do that.' If I hadn't, I don't know how we could have carried on.

At the end of the war, the Colonial Government started various schemes to encourage more young Europeans to come and settle in Kenya. Many young men put their names down for jobs as farm managers. My father interviewed one of them. He wanted him to come and work at Deloraine because it was planned that I should go to England and have a holiday. I hadn't been back to England since 1934 and I hadn't been away from Deloraine for more than two or three weeks. This young man was straight out of the Army, but he was from farming stock. He knew nothing about conditions in Kenya, nor could he speak Swahili, so I had to work with him for about six months before I could take my holiday.

During the next twenty years we did sometimes employ European farm managers, but they didn't usually stay long. If they were any good they would leave to get a better job and ultimately to buy a farm of their own. As the Africans became more skilled, I found that I preferred to depend on them without any other help. When the war ended, one of my Italian prisoners sent me a friend, Pietro Tundo, to work for us as a farm mechanic and he stayed many years until he started up his own business as a contractor. He kept all the machinery in order and I could never have managed without him.

At the end of the war, when the men came back to their farms, some felt they were rather out of touch with farming, so some of us got together and started a Young Farmers' Club. Actually we weren't so young; we made the maximum age thirty. We used to have meetings and invite a speaker to give a talk or else we would visit a farm or government station.

I did not take a great part in this as I was thirty in 1946. At first the Young Farmers were all Europeans and when it was suggested that some Africans should join there was opposition from some of the members. Gradually the age limit was reduced and eventually branches were formed in the schools and by that time the schools had become multi-racial. It happened gradually.

While my father was away in England, I broke my arm in a bad fall out hunting at Molo and had to go to hospital in Nairobi. When I came out I went to convalesce with Patience and Edward Windley at Kiambu, where Edward was the District Commissioner. While there, a message came to say that there was trouble at Uplands and he must go immediately. Off he went and he didn't return until evening and he told us there had been a riot. This was one of the first signs of the trouble that was to come.

Loder had gone to the Muthaiga Club as housekeeper, a job for which she was very suitable. She had very strict ideas about the social scale and once, when the club was full and a duke arrived to stay, she was heard to remark: 'Don't know what this place is coming to, there's that A.C. 'oey inside in a room and 'is Grace outside in a tent!' Another time when the Secretary told her a certain lady was expected, she said: 'I'll put the complaint book in 'er room – save 'er walking to the 'all.' Once when I had been staying there I had been bitten by fleas. I told Loder this and she said: ''Oo was 'ere last? Um, Delameres – I don't think they'd 'ave 'ad fleas.' Loder worked at the club until she was seventy-five, when she retired to Harrison House – the East African Women's League home for old pioneers. She died there aged ninety-three.

In 1948 there were elections for the Legislative Council and some people persuaded my father to stand again. This time he was opposed by Michael Blundell and Lady Sidney Farrar. He was rather put out by this as he had never been opposed before. He took the attitude: 'Well, if the people don't want me, they needn't have me.' He refused to do any canvassing but he did address meetings all over the constituency and Michael Blundell and Lady Sidney would also speak. All three candidates would speak on the same day to save the constituents time and trouble. They would draw lots as to who would speak first. Eventually it was Michael who won the seat. My father was disappointed at the time but he realized that he was getting older and people wanted a younger man. He liked Michael and their policies were much the same. They became very friendly and Michael would often come over to Deloraine and discuss problems with my father. Lady Sidney lost her deposit.

5
Time Off in Europe

When I went to Britain on a holiday in 1948 there was still rationing for food and clothes and I wanted to take my friends some of the things that they had not had for years. I embarked on the aeroplane carrying a large bunch of bananas, a ham and a thermos of cream. I could hardly stagger along under it all but the man at the airport said he wouldn't weigh anything I could carry.

I stayed first in London with Moy and David and bought myself a suitable outfit – including boots and breeches for hunting – and I was taken to Ascot. I then went to the Highland Show in Inverness, so I stayed with my father's sister, Constance Cairns, who lived in Nairn. My cousin Walter Buccleuch was staying there too and we went together to the show. Inverness is very hilly and the streets are narrow and it was quite a problem getting the car through the traffic. Eventually Walter decided to park the car and walk. He was well known as a tremendously strong walker and, dressed up in my smart outfit, I found it very difficult to keep up with him. When we arrived at the showground, I was very hot and covered in sweat and my face as red as a beetroot. Walter said: 'The King and Queen are going to be here and I think you ought to be introduced to them.' I protested but he insisted and said that as I was always in Kenya this was a good opportunity. So off I was marched to the tent where the King and Queen were being shown around by the showground officials. The guard on the gate wouldn't let us in, so Walter took me round to the back of the tent, lifted up the canvas and we crawled in, emerging, much to my embarrassment, in the middle of the tent where the King and Queen were. I was protesting all the time; I had on a smart hat and it was very difficult to crawl under the flap of the tent and still look tidy! However, I was duly introduced to the King and Queen and Walter was satisfied. But we must have been a strange sight, coming out from under the canvas.

I went to Germany after that; David had been posted with his regiment there and I went to stay with him and Moy for a few weeks. Germany had hardly recovered from the war and the people were still very hungry. One could see the ravages of war everywhere. The regiment were living in the sumptuous German barracks built by the Nazis and I was shown the officers' mess with a vomitorium adjacent.

I then went to Ireland to the Dublin Horse Show and from there I went north to stay with my cousin Ran Antrim at Glenarm. After that I crossed the sea from Larne to Stranraer in Scotland. My father had very kindly bought me a hunter and I went to stay with Elisabeth Church in a house she had rented near the Buccleuch kennels, where my horse was stabled, so that I could do some hunting.

Petrol rationing was still in force and so we always rode to the meets and back again. I would help the hunt servants, and often lead one or two spare horses as well as my own, sometimes up to fifteen miles. I used sometimes to help clean tack in the kennel stables and learned a great deal from the stud groom. He had been a stableboy in my grandfather's stables and he told me how they used to have to clean all the silver-plated harness and their liveries each time the family went out in the coach, sometimes not getting to bed until the early hours of the morning.

I often rode the hunt horses and let the hunt servants ride mine. My favourite was an enormous German horse that my cousin had captured during the war. He had been wheeler in a gun team. He was very slow and had no mouth, but would plod on and jump anything that he came to. I felt very confident on him. Riding big hunters, being faced with stone walls and timber and negotiating sheep drains and bogs, or mosses as they called them, were all things new to me and I was teased quite a bit. One day I had been jumping the enormous horse in a school and when I dismounted, my knee went out. The doctor's surgery was just next door, so I hobbled round with my cousin, John Scott, who was the Master. There was a queue of people waiting to see him but my cousin took me past them all saying in a loud voice to the doctor: 'This is my cousin from Africa. She is used to being carried around by four niggers, but since she came here she has had to use her legs, and they have given way under her!'

I stayed in Scotland until the beginning of 1949; then I went back to the farm and settled down to work once again. I brought with me from Scotland a pair of Border terriers and I bred from these for some years afterwards. Alas, there were too many hazards for such game little dogs in Africa and the calamity rate was very high.

In 1950 the Duke and Duchess of Gloucester came out to Kenya to give Nairobi its charter as a city and they stayed with us beforehand. My father hadn't been very well and it was unfortunate that while they were with us he suddenly had a heart attack and had to be taken to hospital in Nakuru. However, he picked up and I was able to accompany the Gloucesters to Nairobi where we stayed with Sir Philip Mitchell and his wife at Government House and I attended the celebrations with them. The Government were a little worried about anti-colonial agitation and there was a sudden scare when we were sitting on the dais in front of the Nairobi City Council building. There was a rush of people in the crowd, a sudden turmoil – but it was only that some people had climbed a tree in order to get a better view and had been attacked by a swarm of bees.

Just after this, I had a rather good thoroughbred hunter, Atomico, and I decided to enter him in the Kenya Grand National. I had sent him away to a professional trainer so that he could work with other horses of his class and get sharpened up a little. I had engaged a good amateur jockey to ride him and he had a fair chance of winning. A few days before the race I was schooling a very wild young horse at Deloraine over some hurdles; the horse hit them hard and we came down. I broke a rib and scraped some skin off my face and so had to go to the hospital in Nakuru. Treatment consisted of having a piece of gauze wrapped right around my face with two holes for my eyes. When the day came for the race, I was desperate to go but the doctor didn't want me to. He said it would be very dusty and I might get some infection in the wound. However, I pleaded with him and eventually he said I might go if I would agree to having my whole head covered in a white lint hood. I agreed and attended the race looking like a member of the Klu-Klux-Klan. It was worth it; my horse won.

After his heart attack my father was not at all strong and he had to keep very quiet for a long time. Gradually, however, he regained some of his strength and in 1952 he went to England for another holiday. Then one day in July I went to stay the night before hunting with some friends near Molo. We had just come in from hunting when the telephone rang. It was Loder on the line from Nairobi and she told me that she had just heard that my father had died in England. It was a shock but not altogether unexpected. My brother-in-law was at that time commanding his regiment at Windsor and the Queen was to present them with a new standard. Afterwards she was to have lunch with Moy and David and the other officers. My father had been invited and he had set off to join them for the lunch party. He went to catch the train at Paddington Station where he had another heart attack and died. Moy and David didn't know this had happened and went on with their lunch party. Later the Queen wrote Moy a very charming letter of condolence in her own hand. He was buried at Minto with my mother.

PART V

A New Start

1
The Mau Mau Emergency

By 1952 we began to hear rumours about Kikuyu taking oaths and of something called Mau Mau - a movement, a society, no one knew what. For some time dead bodies had been found, the bodies of people who had been strangled. And strangled animals were found hanging on gates and fences. Edward Windley was now Provincial Commissioner in Central Province, which included Nairobi; he and others sent in reports to Nairobi but little action was taken. Sir Philip Mitchell went on his retirement leave. This was for six months and the new Governor couldn't take his place until this period was over. The murders and strange happenings got worse and worse; I remember one day when I was coming back from hunting in Molo on a cold wet Sunday afternoon, I saw a group of people in the market place in Molo with a man in a brown leather coat addressing them. I asked the African with me who this was and he replied, 'Oh, that's somebody called Jomo Kenyatta.' We did hear that there were meetings going on all round the country but we didn't know why. Occasionally my Kikuyu would come to me and ask me if I knew that there were some 'bad people' going round but in general everyone seemed to be behaving quite normally. It didn't change life much at that stage.

The new Governor was Sir Evelyn Baring. By the time he arrived things had really become quite bad. A number of people had been murdered. Cattle had been mutilated. The first action he took was to declare a state of emergency in the country and he had a large number of people arrested on the same night, including Jomo Kenyatta. I happened to be staying with Geraldine and Michael Macoun at the time, in Arusha, Tanganyika, where Michael was in charge of the district police. On hearing the news, I hurried home to Deloraine.

Our mountain forests in Kenya have always been a place of refuge for people in trouble. They are extensive and dense, and it is easy to hide there. As there is plenty of good water in the streams and much game, there is little difficulty in getting enough to eat. Some of the plants that grow there make good vegetables and the animals' skins can be used to make clothes. So it was to the forests that many Kikuyu went when they realized that the Government was going to take strong action against them.

Though I have known and liked many Kikuyu, I find it difficult to understand what drove so many of them to do the things they did. Before the advent of colonialism they had been expanding their system of shifting cultivation and they had been gradually moving westward towards the Rift Valley. When the Colonial Government took over, they could no longer do this. Many of them had become squatters on European farms but as time progressed and the Europeans developed their farms these squatters had become more and more restricted until they were only allowed to cultivate half an acre each and keep no cattle. Meanwhile their families were expanding rapidly and they began to feel the pinch. Perhaps it mattered as much that many of them by this time had some education; some had been abroad and seen the world. They had met all kinds of people and had picked up all kinds of foreign ideas. I can't think that any people like being ruled by an alien race, especially if the natives are subject to various restrictions that do not apply to their rulers, as was the case in Kenya. All this I can understand; they were comprehensible grievances. But was it really necessary for them to sink to such depths of degradation in an attempt to improve their lot as some of the Kikuyu did? Was it essential for them to take such depraved oaths at obscene ceremonies as we heard they did?

I had several family ties with the Barings: Evelyn's elder half-brother, Lord Cromer, had married my mother's sister Ruby, and Molly Baring was my second cousin. Her grandfather, Lord Grey, was the brother of my grandmother, Mary Minto. Molly was about eight years older than I, and I had inherited her nanny when I was a baby. The Barings were terribly kind to me and I used to stay with them at Goverment House very often. Molly was a devoted gardener and made the gardens at Government House very beautiful. Evelyn was a very keen farmer; he loved the land and livestock, sheep in particular. He was also a climber and he would often go off to Leukenia, about thirty miles from Nairobi, for rock climbing. His other recreation was bird-watching. He was a good linguist and would try to learn the different languages in the places he had worked in. He could speak some Indian dialects as well as Afrikaans and he and Molly both started learning Swahili when they came to Kenya. Molly also took lessons from Doctor Louis Leakey in Kikuyu. They were both very devout Christians.

Evelyn was essentially a man who wanted to see a country develop, so it was very painful for him to be flung into a country that was in political turmoil, where he had to take stern measures and sign numerous death warrants. He was not physically strong, as his liver had been damaged when in India by an attack of amoebic dysentery. Many of the settlers pressed him to take much harsher measures against the Kikuyu; some even went so far as to say 'Shoot the lot!' But he was convinced that the only way to stop the insurrection was to encourage those Kikuyu who did not support the Mau Mau. Foremost amongst these were those who were Christian. Evelyn believed that these people must be given all the support we could and that it was only the Kikuyu who could defeat the Mau Mau elements in their tribe. He was sometimes accused of being weak but he was firm in holding his beliefs and acting on them.

It was during his term that the Swynnerton Plan was put into force. The Kikuyu had previously lived in scattered holdings. This plan consolidated the Kikuyu holdings and gathered them into villages. It also obliged them to take to more modern farming practices. Since there was an official state of emergency, the Government had the power to make people do things which it wouldn't normally have been able to do.

It wasn't only the settlers who were asking for sterner measures. I remember my head Masai telling me that if he were the Government he would collect all the Kikuyu together, put them in an enclosure, pour petrol over them, then send an aeroplane with a bomb and drop it on them and do in the lot! Of course not all settlers had extreme views and many of them supported Evelyn and his policies. He had a number of Kikuyu servants working in Government House who were kept on all through the emergency. I think that he thought – just as I did – that it wouldn't be right to discharge people who had done no known wrong and who had worked well for a number of years. I too kept my Kikuyu house servants all through the emergency. It was true that many Europeans who had trusted their servants were let down and found them to be among the most rabid of the Mau Mau. There were several very grisly murders of Europeans in which their servants had clearly colluded if not taken part.

Many Europeans became very nervous and would lock themselves into their houses at night, barricading the doors so that nobody could get in and enclosing the verandahs with steel mesh wire. I felt I would suffer from claustrophobia. I just left the house open as usual though I did have wire netting over the windows. I put a Masai to sleep on the veranda and I thought that if anybody came to attack me, they would have to attack him first and I would get warning. I always carried a small Beretta pistol which had been given me by David Smiley. All Europeans were supposed to carry weapons and tie them to their persons with a lanyard. I never used to load mine except at night, when I kept it loaded by my bed. I cannot say that I was ever seriously frightened during this time. But as the Kikuyu on our farm were a minority there really wasn't much risk; it was not like some farms which had an almost one hundred per cent Kikuyu labour force. Such farms had great difficulties because at times the security forces would swoop down on them and arrest their entire labour force, leaving them with nobody.

Once a state of emergency had been declared, all kinds of restrictions were put on Kikuyu which did not affect any other people. Some of our Kikuyu announced that they wished to go back to the Kikuyu reserve, even though some of them had never been there in their lives. I arranged for some lorries to transport them to Nakuru where there was a transit camp for such people. I told them they could go but they must never come back because I would never give them back their jobs. Most of our Kikuyu said they would like to stay on the farm. We had very little trouble; the only incident was that one old man was found hanging from a tree. It was never explained.

All the European men and some of the non-Kikuyu Africans were enlisted into the Kenya Police Reserve. They were often called out at night to raid different villages and farms to see if there was anyone there who was not supposed to be. Occasionally they would catch somebody. Once a man took them into the forest near us and showed them where the rest of his gang was hiding; they shot one person who was trying to run away but it turned out to be a woman dressed up in a greatcoat. Sometimes the European men would tell me that they were sickened by the things they saw.

I also joined the Police Reserve but all I ever did was occasionally to go down to the police station and sort out cards containing people's confessions of what oaths they had taken. The ones I saw merely said: 'I will fight for my land, I will not drink beer, I will not sleep with prostitutes' but later some Kikuyu took some very disgusting oaths. It was hard to see how anyone who had taken such oaths and had taken part in the ceremonies that went with them would ever be able to mix again with their fellows in any human society.

My remaining Kikuyu had to be 'screened'. This consisted of interrogation as to whether they had taken oaths. This was done by some of the Europeans who were thought to be conversant with Kikuyu ways, helped by some Kikuyu loyalists. They would take my people off in batches.

Sometimes they would come back with bumps and bruises and even cigarette burns on them. I used to be rather annoyed and I told them that I thought it was wrong that they had been treated like this. However, they said: 'No, it was quite right. If they don't do this to us, how can they find out if we have taken any oaths or not?' Then they roared with laughter and started describing how one very fat man – cook to one of my neighbours – had behaved. He was made to do numerous press-ups and had moaned and groaned. They thought this a great joke. Not one single person was arrested from Deloraine, but I think that was quite unusual.

Life on the farm during the emergency really went on as before. Occasionally there would be a rumour that someone had spotted a Mau Mau and then all the men would rush out to attack the intruder, seizing any weapon they could lay their hands on, a fencing dropper or a rock. The women would all come rushing towards my house with their children and when I asked what they were doing they would say: 'Well, if you're going to be killed, we would like to be there with you.' What exactly they meant, I didn't inquire. This only happened once or twice. We had plenty of other labour and so we were not really inconvenienced at all.

Moy and David had bought some land on the Kinangop to retire to when he left the Army and I used to look after this for them. Three of my Kikuyu had gone up there to work. These three had refused to take oaths and the local people had told them they would come and kill them. It was very thick forest all round the house. One day one of them was attacked, slashed with a panga and left for dead. He was rushed to hospital in time and eventually recovered. The European family who were renting the house at the time had been given a young RAF airman with a rifle to protect them. One day the other two Kikuyu were walking down to the river to start the water pump. They were carrying a gun, which they had permission to do, and this young RAF boy, who was newly out from England, did not know who they were, fired at them and hit one through the leg and the other through the stomach. Of course he was horrified when he discovered who they were. He was only about nineteen and burst into tears. This kind of accident happened often. All Europeans had weapons, even old ladies who had no idea how to handle guns. It was quite dangerous at a dinner party when each person put his gun down beside his plate pointing across the table at the person on the other side. There were many mishaps.

Terrible things did happen in the emergency; there were atrocities on both sides. Some of the Europeans would see red when they saw what the Mau Mau had done. Whole communities were massacred, men, women and children slashed and hacked to pieces. Many more Kikuyu were killed than Europeans and the so-called loyalists, the Kikuyu Home Guard, were the most bitter of all. A stage was reached when most of the Mau Mau had taken refuge in the forests and it was very difficult to round them up. Some British regiments came out to Kenya; they had been trained to jungle warfare, but they were quite strange to the forests and the forest noises and the animals startled them. So some of the younger European Kenyans formed what were known as 'pseudo-gangs'.

Many of the older Europeans could not speak Swahili well enough to carry on a general conversation with an African. Most of them had been more interested in their farming than in learning local languages but some of the younger generation who had been born and brought up in Kenya had spent their childhood playing with African children and hunting with them, going into the forest with bows and arrows and looking for honey. They could often speak the language fluently. They knew how to track and how to move in the forest. They dressed themselves up like the Mau Mau in skins and went barefoot. First they had to segregate themselves from the European community for quite some time and not wash in order to smell like the Mau Mau. Then together with some ex-Mau Mau they would go into the forests and locate the Mau Mau gangs, lay ambushes for them and capture them. They were very brave, because even though they had blacked faces and were disguised as convincingly as possible, it was quite easy for them to be spotted and if caught they would have been killed straightaway. Many of them could speak Kikuyu, but there were others who couldn't. I think these people were instrumental in eventually getting rid of the last remnants of the Mau Mau in the forests.

Gradually the movement was overcome; it had petered out by about 1956 but there were thousands of people in detention camps who had to be sorted out and released slowly. Only about thirty Europeans were killed, whereas about ten thousand Kikuyu died. Virtually all the Mau Mau were Kikuyu, although occasionally a man from another tribe joined them. I think the other tribes sympathized in some of their aims, such as abolishing the colour bar in schools and hospitals, ending the different rates of wages and restrictions in land ownership, but they didn't agree with oath-taking and the strangling and other atrocities.

2

Spreading the News

After my father died, I had a little more money and I sometimes had a European working on the farm, which meant I could get away more easily. In 1953 and 1954 I went to stay with some friends, Peter and Yvonne Molloy, in Juba, Sudan. He was a game warden. I motored up, staying one night in a Government rest house in Uganda. My driver at that time was a Masai and I took another Masai to keep him company. They did not at all approve of the *Il Lemek* (uncircumcised) Nilotics who lived in those parts, especially as they went around naked. The Sudanese used to call the Masai 'Maumau' which they didn't like either.

We went on safaris with the Molloys into some very wild bush and Yvonne shot an elephant. I had no wish to do this, so I would stay in camp when the Molloys were after elephant. One day my Masai came to me and asked me whether it was more difficult to shoot an elephant or a snake. I said that I supposed shooting an elephant would be more difficult, but they said 'No, an elephant is a huge thing that no one could miss, whereas a snake is only as thick as a finger.' The Sudanese must have asked them why I didn't shoot elephants like Yvonne and to keep face they had replied that I sometimes shot snakes!

In 1955 I went to Europe and stayed with Moy and David in Stockholm where David was Military Attaché. In 1956 I did a trip round Lake Kivu in what was then the Belgian Congo. This is an area of spectacular scenery, snow-clad mountains, hot lava flows and lakes. We met the tall Watutsi tribe and the little Pygmies. It is a very rich and beautiful part of the world.

In 1959 I flew to Durban and stayed with various friends in Natal, and I then took a bus from Pietermaritzburg to Bulawayo in Southern Rhodesia, as it was then. After staying with some friends there, I flew back to Kenya from Salisbury. I do not like the South African racial attitude nor the way they run their country but I found South Africa very interesting because many of their birds, beasts, vegetation and indeed peoples are so like ours. In a way I felt at home there – but the Europeans there were astonished when they heard that I lived alone on a farm and managed a labour force of a hundred men. Most of the European women there have been brought up to be frightened of Africans, especially the men, and would never have stayed alone on a farm.

I was looking after the farm all this time and more and more, in a small way, getting involved in various ways of sharing ideas about farming and development. First, there was the Farmers' Association. Each district in the settled areas of Kenya had its own association. They had begun as associations to put forward the Kenya settlers' point of view. Ours was the Rongai Valley Farmers' Association. All the European farmers in the area belonged to it and we would take turns as chairman and at sitting on the Executive Committee. It was my turn to take the chair from 1954 to 1958. We discussed things like the use of rivers, repairs to roads, cattle quarantines and such like. People would give us talks at our meetings, which we held about once a month; they came from the creameries, the Kenya Meat Commission, the Labour Department or the plant breeders and often they were very interesting. Most of the members were very conservative in their outlook and hated anything new, particularly any new regulations brought out by the Government, and especially those to do with labour. Sometimes they would get quite worked up about a new regulation which they thought impossible to implement, such as having to build houses for labourers with walls eight foot high. Many of these farmers lived where there were only acacia trees and they got into a great state about this; how could they build houses with walls eight feet high out of acacia trees, as no acacias had straight trunks that high? Then disputes would arise: one member who had land on the lower reaches of a river would complain that the member above him was taking all the water; or perhaps someone's stock was walking through someone else's land on the way to the railway station and spreading disease. Roads were always a bone of contention, as to who was responsible for their upkeep. People became quite excited over these issues; I remember somebody arriving rather late and saying he hadn't heard what the last speaker said but whatever it was, he opposed it! On another occasion I recall someone taking off his coat and saying: 'I don't agree with the last speaker and if he will take off his coat I am ready to meet him outside.' However, these little arguments didn't usually last long and as a rule we had a friendly cup of tea and gossip after the meeting.

Nearly all these people had created their farms out of raw Africa. Most of them had no money except what they had worked for. Their labour force had been illiterate, untrained Africans. There were no guidelines in the early days on running a farm and everything had been achieved through trial and error. By now the land had been developed into highly productive farms with heavy-milking dairy cows, pigs, steers and good crops of wheat and maize. Farm workers had been trained and some had become skilled and responsible. To create anything is satisfactory, and it wasn't surprising that people became possessive and resented what they thought might interfere with their achievements.

Then in 1958 I was asked by the Provincial Commissioner of Nakuru to sit on the District Agricultural Committee in Baringo District which was just north of us, outside the European area. He said that since I was a woman, I would be a good example to the Africans. The Committee was composed of both officials – the District Commissioner, who was the chairman, and the District Agricultural, Livestock and Forestry Officers as well as some junior officers – and non-officials such as the Chiefs, and other leaders of the district. Sometimes we held our meetings in a Government office, but we used to visit all the different parts of the country to see what was going on; often we would camp out and hold our meetings under shady trees. The Baringo District is very large, stretching right up into the desert country in the North. Some of it is very arid and difficult and the Tugen hills, which divide the Rift Valley from the Kerio Valley, are precipitous, with sections rising over 9,000 feet.

Most of the people who live in these parts are Tugen. They are agricultural as well as pastoral and speak Kalenjin. In the middle of this area is Lake Baringo, a fresh-water lake with a large and varied population of water birds that is home to a number of hippos and crocodiles. The people round Lake Baringo are not Tugen but Ilchamu (or Njemps) who are an offshoot of the Laikipiak Masai. They are said to be one of the sections which disappeared after the Laikipiak Masai were defeated and dispersed. When they settled by the lake, they had no cattle and so were forced to eat fish, which is anathema to the Masai proper, who say that eating fish is the same as eating snakes. The Ilchamu also eat water lily roots and other plants that grow in or near the lake and they have learnt how to make boats, which they propel with little paddles very much like ping-pong bats. But being Masai they still wanted cattle. One of them told me how when they first arrived they wondered how they could get cattle. The people living around them, the Tugen and the Pokot, kept cattle. The Ilchamu had by that time learnt to swim and one day when they were splashing about in the water they said to the Tugen, who were herding their cattle on the shore, 'Why don't you come into the water? It's lovely.' To which the cattle herders replied that it was dangerous and they might drown. The Ilchamu promised they wouldn't and enticed them into the water – whereupon they promptly sank (perhaps with a little help) and the Ilchamu scrambled out of the water and took their cattle.

Another story they told me was about a battle with their neighbours, the Tugen. There were a lot of little wild plants in that area which after the rains had nasty thorns which got into your feet. The Ilchamu said to the Tugen: 'Let us fight without shoes.' Not knowing about the thorns the Tugen agreed. The Ilchamu put on very thin sandals which the Tugen didn't notice. When they fought the Tugen were immobilized by the thorns and the Ilchamu were again able to take their cattle.

Up in the hills where the Tugen live, it is quite fertile country but very steep. I think they were pushed up there by the Masai, who grazed all the better land lower down. The biggest problem in the Baringo District in my day was overstocking. The Masai used to raid the Tugen cattle and keep the numbers down but with the advent of colonial rule this had to stop. When the grass was finished, they could no longer move on; they were forced to stay in the same area. Then inoculations for cattle caused the numbers to grow and grow until the land could not support them any longer; it became so heavily over-grazed that the grass would not grow even after the rains. The rainfall in this area is fairly heavy and the water would wash away the top soil and big gullies would appear. The problem was how to restore the grass and keep the cattle down to reasonable numbers. Africans hate destocking because, they say, if you keep many cattle, you can afford to lose some. If you have a hundred cows and fifty die in a drought you still have fifty left. Africans count their wealth in cattle and as they lead very simple lives the people of Baringo had little desire for money, so they were very reluctant to sell off any stock. However, the Government made sale yards and held sales every few months and the people were forced to sell. Cattle would be picked out by the headman, branded and brought to the sale yard.

Meanwhile, we had a system of rehabilitating the land. We would divide an area into four sections. Everyone had to put their cattle into one of these four sections, which would be grazed for four months; then they all moved their cattle onto the next section and grazed that for four months, and so on. It took sixteen months to get round all four sections which gave each section a full year to seed and regenerate. The main objection to this system was that people had built their huts all over the place and they had patches of millet or maize near their homes, so it meant a long trek every day for some of them to fetch their milk. There was also much erosion on the hillsides because they had cultivated on such steep land. They were supposed to build terraces but this was difficult and they didn't like it.

We used to go through lists of people who were to be given loans in order to buy grade cattle or a tractor and we had to be careful that the names on the list weren't all relations of the members of the Committee! We also built cattle dips, and that was a problem, because dips need water and water was often very short. There were some dams and bore holes but, more often than not, the pumps had broken down and the money allocated by the Government for their upkeep was finished and so they couldn't be mended until the next financial year. This meant that people who had good cattle could not dip or had to walk their cattle a long way, often through infected stock, to reach the next dip.

We were also trying to introduce a system of individual land tenure. Under the old African system, most land was communal and this meant nobody had real responsibility for it. As soon as land was worn out, they simply moved on elsewhere. Even if anyone tried to reserve some grass for dry weather, they couldn't stop their neighbours from coming in and grazing it. In Baringo we were aiming for an organized system of individual tenure with title deeds. When the land had recovered under the four section system, we would divide it into individual holdings of an economic size and people would be given a plot and issued with the title deeds. The land would be surveyed and this meant people owned their own land and nobody else could interfere with it. This system had remarkable results and we soon found people were enclosing areas for themselves without proper survey so that they could develop their land without interference.

It was around this time that I first met Daniel arap Moi, later the President. He was then a member of the Legislative Council and used to come to our meetings occasionally because his constituency was in the Baringo area. Baringo was a closed district which meant that anyone entering it had to have a permit from the Provincial Commissioner. The main reason for this was that it was dry in many parts and people would often set off in little cars, without sufficient water or petrol, and would break down and have to be rescued. This was dangerous for themselves and a nuisance for the administration. And it was also convenient to be able to keep out poachers, agitators and religious fanatics. The result was that many Europeans, even those living close by, had never been in the closed district. Several of the Rongai European farmers never had, and consequently they took very little interest in what was going on. Some, if you talked to them about it, would say: 'Well, I'd be more interested if the people would come out and work; all they seem to do is laze about and drink beer.' Again, Europeans who lived near the border of the Tugen country suffered badly from the Tugen bringing their cattle onto their farms, dropping infected ticks and poaching their grass and water – and sometimes going home with some of the cattle. As can be imagined this did not endear them to the Europeans, though more and more were employed as labour and often had a very good relationship with the farmers.

I stayed on this Committee six years – until 1964 when the rules were changed – and I received a very nice letter from the Agricultural Officer. He explained that in future members would have to be elected from registered inhabitants of the district so that of course I was now ineligible. He went on: 'But on behalf of Baringo, I would like to thank you for your work and friendship for the farmers of the district. It was extremely valuable to us to have a large scale farmer of your experience on the Committee – especially one like you, who would visit and know people and out of the way places, as you did.'

I found the work in Baringo very interesting, as it gave me an insight into the problems of the people and land that I would not have had otherwise, and also some experience of how the Government administered a district of that kind.

3
Enlarging the Farm

I had by now lived so long in the Great Rift Valley that I felt I was part of it. I had learned to know its moods and habits. In the dry weather the skies took on a brassy look – all the vegetation would shrivel up, the leaves would drop from the trees, the dams would dry up and there would be nothing for the cattle to eat. Then clouds of dust would blow, whirlwinds spiral into the sky and great black clouds gather, the thunder would crackle and roar – and at last rain would fall, bringing with it the sweet smell of fresh wet earth. In only two or three days magical sprouts of green would appear and before I knew it I would be waging a war against weeds of all kinds. Sometimes it seemed as if the rain would never stop; everything would be flooded and we had to be ceaselessly on the lookout for erosion in the fields. Bridges would be washed away and roads would become impassable. Africa never does things by halves. Farmers had to get used to the very erratic rainfall; some years we would get rain all through the year, some hardly any at all. Our rainfall at Deloraine varied from twenty-three inches in one year to fifty-six inches in another with an average of thirty-eight. Sometimes it rained in January; sometimes it didn't rain till August, though March or April was the usual time for the rains to start. Every year we would get a long spell of dry weather and all we could do was wait for the rains; it often felt as though they would never come and we would wonder how we should be able to keep the cattle fed. By this time, admittedly, we cut a lot of hay for the cattle but it was almost impossible to cut enough for the large number we had. If we reduced the cattle to the number that could be fed through a very dry period, we would have far too few during the wet period. So it was very difficult to get the right balance.

In 1960 we had a terrible drought which was then followed by floods. Worse still, we had an infestation of army worm. Conditions were apparently just right for these infamous insects. They must have laid their eggs in the ground some years before and when conditions were suitable they all hatched out. Everything was covered with them; they ate up all the new grass that came up with the rains after the long drought. The cattle had virtually nothing to eat; some of them ate the army worms and a number of them lay down and died. It was a very distressing sight.

Sometimes my heart would fill with despair, and I would climb up the hill at the back of the farm and sit on a rock. My mother had done the same when she was depressed, forty years before. Here I could look over the wide expanse of the Rift. If I looked to the south I knew that there was nothing there but the Masai steppes, and I could visualize their herds of cattle and their *manyattas* stretching right down to the middle of Tanganyika. Then I would turn to look towards the north, and there I would see the hills stretching away until they were out of sight. There the country is all desert, and I could picture the nomads driving their stock through the dust, looking for pasture and water. They might only water their cattle once in three days and then the water would all have to be lifted up by hand, little by little, from deep wells. Then I would let my eyes rest on the land directly below me. This was the so-called White Highlands, at this point only about thirty to forty miles wide. There I would see a railway line that carried goods from the sea to Uganda in the heart of Africa, and parallel with it a metalled road by which it was possible to cross to the other side of Africa and the Atlantic Ocean. I could see a line of electric pylons bringing power from the River Nile. If you looked more closely, you would see that the land had been cleared of bush, and was planted with crops of wheat and maize. Dairy cows were grazing on the grass leys with water laid on to each field and here and there was a solidly built stone house. Then I would remember that less than a century ago this land had carried little but herds of antelope, and I would take courage and feel that perhaps, after all, something worthwhile had been achieved.

After the war the Government had tried to bring out as many settlers as possible and some of the large farms had been bought up by the Ministry of Settlement and divided into smaller units; it was thought it would be more productive to farm the land more intensively. By the Sixties there were many very beautiful, well-run farms in the Highlands but by then it had become obvious that Kenya couldn't go on as it was. There was bound to be political change. Africans wanted a bigger say in government and they wanted more land. At the same time, the British Government didn't seem interested in having colonies any more.

A series of conferences was held in England to decide what kind of constitution we should have. In Kenya the European settlers were divided. Those led by Sir Ferdinand Cavendish-Bentinck thought that changes towards African rule must be resisted at every step. They thought there would be no future for the country if the Africans were in control. Others, led by Michael Blundell, recognized that it was useless to swim against the tide and resist change; it was inevitable that Africans should take a leading part in the country. When Michael Blundell formed the New Kenya Party, his supporters were only about twenty per cent European; Asians and Africans made up the rest.

Land ownership was the big problem. In pre-colonial days it was essential for an African to have access to land because he had no other means of livelihood and almost every African in the Sixties still regarded land as something which he could not do without. Once there had been plenty and everyone moved freely to make use of it. Now some Europeans owned many thousands of acres, mostly under grass. To many Africans – at least those with agricultural traditions like the Kikuyu – land that wasn't cultivated seemed wasted. In their view cattle should graze only in areas that were unsuitable for crops, such as steep and rocky hillsides or swamp. Land under grass seemed to them under-utilized, even if it did produce milk, meat and wool. On the other hand, most Europeans had developed their farms to a high standard and some of them had been held in the same families for two or more generations. They had usually put everything they possessed into their land and many of them had nothing else in the world. The younger generations who had been born and bred on these farms had often never lived anywhere else and knew no other kind of life. So when they were threatened by change, they became extremely worried. They were used to dealing with adversity; they knew how to tighten their belts and wait for better times. But now they felt as though the world had been swept from beneath their feet and they were powerless to do anything. Many Europeans were afraid that once an African Government gained control, they would expropriate the farms without compensation and many people would thereby be ruined.

The British Government organized a scheme by which British farmers could be bought out and paid with money in England. This would enable them to start life elsewhere. The land that was bought was then to be divided and distributed to landless Africans. This meant that some of the large farms would be divided into smallholdings of only a few acres, of a size considered suitable as one economic unit. Nobody was to be forced to sell. The Europeans then had to decide what to do, whether to sell up or stay. Many of them felt that they were being offered a reasonable price and could not refuse it. Some had children to be educated and they felt it too big a risk to stay where they were. Others felt more confidence in the future and decided not to sell. People were divided into 'stayers' and 'goers'. If the majority of people in a district decided to sell, even those who wanted to stay felt it would be very difficult if they were to be surrounded by small peasant farms. The facilities they had previously enjoyed would no longer continue; clubs would go certainly, perhaps telephones, water and roads, and they would be forced to sell. In some cases they were already harassed by Africans who started stealing their cattle and fencing wire and chopping down their trees. Many Europeans felt that it was no good staying on under these conditions. Sometimes parties of Africans would come and ask if they could buy the land. The farmer might think, or even say: 'I don't want to sell but I suppose I shall have to.' And then before he had made up his mind, another party of Africans would hear about it and decide that if he was going to sell they had better get the land before somebody else did. Then they invaded the farm and started ploughing it up and building their houses before the farmer had actually agreed to sell. These kind of happenings were very alarming and more and more Europeans decided to sell.

It was heart-rending for some of them to know that all their work would be destroyed: the fences would come down, the cattle would be sold and the whole place divided up into small plots. The Africans on the other hand wanted security; they wanted somewhere where they could live because if a man had no land and no work he was lost. They wanted a piece of land on which they could build themselves a house and grow enough food for their families and possibly grow cash crops to pay for expenses like school fees and clothes.

Some of the Europeans who made the decision to sell decided to go to Southern Rhodesia or South Africa, others to Australia and some even thought of going to South America. It was a very difficult decision for them, especially for the young people who had never lived anywhere but Kenya. It meant starting a completely new life.

It was in these circumstances that in 1962 my neighbour Mrs Chester decided that she would have to sell her farm. The Chesters had changed their name from Kevster to Chester during the war, having come from Breslau in what was then the eastern part of Germany. Their land there had been taken after the war by the Russians. They had received no compensation and Mrs Chester's family persuaded her that it was too big a risk to stay at Fintry (once the Sladens' farm). Her husband had died some years earlier and by now she was over seventy. So reluctantly she agreed to sell. I decided that I must buy her land. We were very close, the houses and farm buildings were not more than four hundred yards apart and the streams and road and everything were connected to each other. I felt that disagreeable neighbours at Fintry would make Deloraine intolerable. Everybody told me that I was mad and nobody would help me, but I decided that I would have to bring out to Kenya the little money that my father had left me in England, just when everybody else was sending their money out of the country. But I did manage to get a sixty per cent loan from the Government and was able to buy this land. It made Deloraine a much better unit. It came to about 5,000 acres altogether. I took on Mrs Chester's labour – most of them were related to my people – but I didn't take any of the loose assets such as the cattle. This laid a big burden on me financially as the land was not well developed and I had to do a lot of work on it. We made a fairly large dam and this eased the water situation considerably, as water had always been a problem at Deloraine.

Soon after I had bought Fintry, I made an interesting discovery. I noticed that in the area near the springs whenever we dug a hole for a fence post we unearthed a number of pottery fragments, as well as pieces of animal bones. I took these to the University of Nairobi and showed them to some archaeologists, who later came and did a dig. It appeared that there were innumerable earthen pots containing bones, almost as though people had been cooking food and had had to abandon it in a hurry. Furthermore, they found a human skeleton buried in an upright sitting position with its hands on its knees. This, I am told, is a very unusual position for burial. It appeared to have been put in a hole which was then filled in. It was the skeleton of an immature person. Since then some other people have done digs, and they tell me that the pots that they have found are unlike any others that have been found in other parts of Kenya; some of them have flat bottoms and spouts.

The skeleton was carbon-dated A.D. 850. I was told that this was the only find of that millennium to have been discovered in the Rift Valley. Most of the artifacts that have been found in Kenya are thousands of years B.C., and relatively modern history can be explained only by oral tradition. Obsidian tools are very commonly found at Deloraine, and in most parts of the Rift Valley, and we have found large lumps of obsidian here which must have been brought here from an obsidian mine about thirty miles away as a stock for flaking off new tools. There are so many archaeological sites in the Rift Valley that it is difficult for the researchers to know which to work on first, and money to pay for the work is hard to come by; so sadly only a very little work has been done here.

4
Citizen of Kenya

In the early Sixties there was still a wide social gulf between the races and so I thought it would be fun to start a debating society that would bring people in Rongai together. I persuaded some of the European farmers to come once a week and meet people like the post office staff and the railway and health people. We debated all kinds of things. I remember once the subject was 'Is bribery a good thing?' One of the Africans argued that it was, because if Judas Iscariot had not been bribed by the Jews, Christ would not have been crucified, and none of us would have been saved! People would come and give talks on all kinds of topics, careers, trips overseas, and so on, and afterwards we had tea together. It was quite popular for a while but gradually people lost interest.

When Independence came, on 12 December 1963, I was not asked to any of the official celebrations and I stayed at home at Deloraine. I lay awake in bed till midnight. I had at that time a tame hyrax; he was sitting on the roof that night and when he heard the big cheer that came up from the African village he began to screech, which I thought was rather fitting; it was as though he was celebrating too. I could only lie in bed and pray that all would be well. Our President, Jomo Kenyatta, who had once been described to us as 'a leader into darkness and death', took immediate steps to allay the fears of Europeans. He felt it very important that there should be stability in the country and this would be impossible if all the Europeans suddenly disappeared. He called a meeting of the settlers and said what he could to calm their fears. We were given two years in which to decide whether we wanted to become Kenyan citizens or not. I had no doubts. I knew I wanted to be a Kenyan, because all my interests were in Kenya and I felt that I was a Kenyan already. I really had few links with Britain or anywhere else and I wanted to be part of Kenya, for better or worse. I applied for citizenship as soon as I possibly could and Daniel arap Moi was kind enough to sign my papers. By April 1964 the whole procedure was complete and I think I was one of the earliest Europeans to take citizenship. Many others waited until the two years were nearly up before they decided what to do and others never became citizens because their applications were not acknowledged. Many people tried to persuade me against becoming a citizen, telling me I should no longer have the support of the British Government; I might be detained; my land might be confiscated; and all manner of dreadful things might happen. I am glad to say that none of these things did happen and I have always been very glad that I did become a Kenyan in law as I felt I was in fact.

No doubt it was easier for me, being on my own with no dependants, to make such an important decision. But personally I never felt very worried about the future. I always felt that Kenya would make progress without too much trouble. Most Africans appeared from the start to be most welcoming and pleased that I had sufficient confidence in the future of the country to become a citizen and soon I was asked to join various committees. When I showed reluctance, as I had many other things to do, they would tell me: 'No, you are a Kenyan, and you must pull your weight. You cannot just sit there and do nothing.' So soon I found myself on the Harambee (Self-Help) Committee in Rongai and I had to spend many hours at meetings discussing how we could raise funds to build a secondary school, which we eventually succeeded in doing. Now we have a very good one in Rongai. At the time of Independence only about eight per cent of the children from primary schools in Kenya were able to get into secondary schools because there were so few. So there was a big drive to start Harambee secondary schools. These schools were not run with any Government aid, but entirely by voluntary subscriptions. Some of them were badly managed but ours, thanks to the support of the Catholic Mission, who have provided both teachers and funds, has turned into a very good school.

One day we had a funds drive and Daniel arap Moi kindly consented to be the guest of honour. At that time he was Vice-President of Kenya. The members of the committee were lined up to be introduced to him. I was the only European and when the African chairman came to me, he said 'This one looks white, but never mind, she is black at heart!'

I was also on the District Education Board in Nakuru. There were about 230 primary schools in the Nakuru District with about 130,000 pupils. That makes over 500 children to a school. Sitting on a committee of this sort gave me a much better insight into the problems of the ordinary people. Even today, as a European, I find myself rather segregated from the people.

In 1965 the Minister of Agriculture appointed me to the Board of Governors of Egerton College. This college was started on land donated by Lord Egerton of Tatton. His original idea was to train European settlers as farmers, but when it became obvious that there were going to be few European farmers left and that most of the farmers were going to be Africans, the college started admitting African students. Now there are over a thousand of them, from many other African countries as well as Kenya. Outside South Africa, it has the highest standard of any agricultural college in Africa south of the Sahara. At present there are sixteen different courses and the students receive diplomas after completing three years. Graduates of Egerton can be found in positions of responsibility in all parts of the country. Of course, we now have African veterinary officers, agricultural officers, District Commissioners and Provincial Commissioners. No doubt they were young and inexperienced and they had a great challenge to meet, but most of them tried to meet it and they gradually acquired experience. There are still, however, a number of Europeans who come out on short-term contracts as advisers or specialists in certain fields.

To turn a colony into an independent nation was no easy task. All births are accompanied by a certain amount of pain and the birth of a nation is no exception. Kenya, like most of Africa, has gone through a rapid transition. It is only a century – not much longer than a living man's memory will stretch – since its people were living in their simple traditional way, without money or writing, each knowing his place in society. Then their land became a Colonial Dependency, and an alien culture was forced upon them with a new legal system, a new religion, a new economy, a completely new way of life. Then came independence, that is to say political independence, but not financial independence. We are still largely dependent financially on the 'developed countries', all of whom have their own axes to grind. People who raise their hands in desperation and horror at what seems to them incompetence and corruption in Africa should remember this.

In colonial times we were divided into racial categories; we were not citizens but Europeans, Asians, Africans or Natives. Hospitals and schools would accept only those of a specified race. Rates of pay were distinct, as were job categories, and Asians and Africans could only rise to certain levels. It was the custom of the country for hotels and clubs to restrict entry or membership to people of one race. This meant there was very little social contact between the races. When *Uhuru* (Independence) was imminent it became obvious that this racial segregation had to go and Europeans started inviting Asians and Africans to meals in their homes. I remember once being asked to lunch with someone and being told: 'We are asking an African and have placed you next to him, as I know you won't mind.' Of course I didn't, but there were still some people who did. Once a certain lady who found herself placed next to an African at a Government House dinner party got up and walked out.

A question that was asked sometimes at political meetings was: 'Which is better, a dog or a man?' When the answer came 'A man, of course', the questioner would say: 'Then why do Europeans have dogs in their houses, even sitting on their chairs, yet don't allow Africans to do the same?' Social integration was made more difficult by Africans hating fixed invitations for a certain time or day. Very often they would not answer invitations or not turn up on the appointed day; and this in turn made the Europeans disinclined to invite them again. Also, they rarely asked Europeans to their houses: it is not an African custom to hold formal parties except on a special occasion like a wedding. When they visit each other, they turn up at any time of day and do not expect formal invitations. Europeans felt that they could not go to someone's house without an invitation, and so there was little mixing.

When schools that had previously been purely European started admitting children of other races, all kinds of difficulties arose. Very often the Africans were much older than European children of the same educational standard, because they had started school later. Many came from poor families and weren't used to things the European children took for granted, such as pyjamas, toothpaste and toys. Many of them were not used to water-borne sanitation and did not know how to use a European type of lavatory. Sometimes the poor would steal from the rich and when accused they would complain of racialism. Many of the African children were allowed into the expensive schools on bursaries and only paid minimum fees, while the European parents had sometimes to struggle to find the full fees. That too caused resentment.

Hospital integration was not so difficult, although some Europeans didn't like the idea of lying alongside Africans. I remember one lady shuddering at the thought of having a blood transfusion of African blood. Hotels and clubs had to open their doors to everyone and at first there was a certain amount of heart-burning over this, but gradually everyone got used to rubbing shoulders. I am sometimes secretly amused when I see certain people in clubs and hotels quite happily sitting among Africans, and remember how they used to say they would never do such a thing and how it wouldn't be safe to bring their teenage daughters into a place full of young African men.

At the time of Independence and for a few years beforehand, Africans started to take over jobs carrying a responsibility that they would never have hoped for before. So it became imperative that education should be expanded and people should be trained in various skills as quickly as possible. Air travel was organized to take students abroad and many countries gave bursaries to enable students to study in their countries. Furthermore a number of volunteers came here to teach and train the local people. Some of these volunteers were more useful than others; very often they would try and expound a theory that might have been very successful in their own country but was not applicable to African conditions. In fact some were pretty weird! Not many of the young European Kenyans took jobs teaching Africans, and sometimes those who did apply were turned down in case they might have 'colonial attitudes'.

However, Moy's two sons did teach here for a short while. Xan, who later became a journalist, taught in one of the better secondary schools, and Philip taught at a Harambee or 'self-help' school, like ours in Rongai. Some of these schools were of low standards; many with inadequate funds and some with dishonest committees. Sadly, many of the parents who were illiterate themselves didn't realize they were getting little or nothing for the fees they paid and which they had scraped together with great difficulty. Families would club together to get enough money to put one child through, expecting that once he had passed his exams he would get a well-paid job and then in return he would pay fees for the younger members of the families. But some of the better-run Harambee schools were successful and they were gradually taken over by the Government. On the whole they did fill a gap and served a useful purpose.

After Independence, as before, land was the most emotional of all subjects. I have already explained how differently Europeans and Africans looked on land. To a European, it was property, capable of being improved and developed so that it produced wealth. To an African, land was above all security. Now that the old way of life had vanished, a piece of land on which he could build a house and keep his family was all he could fall back on if he hadn't a job. Owing to their old system of shifting cultivation, few Africans had had much idea of improving the land. Now there wasn't enough for everyone – and the Europeans seemed to have much too big a share of it.

At the time of Independence many of the large-scale farms were bought by cooperatives. Several hundred people, usually illiterate, would pool their resources and get a loan from the Kenyan Government and buy a farm, each person taking shares according to how much he had contributed. Until the loan had been repaid, the property had to be run as a large-scale farm, after which it could be divided up into small-scale holdings, according to the number of shares each member help. Unfortunately this sometimes led to corruption. Traditionally Africans had not regarded farming as a business; most of them did not understand economics. Often the managers and directors were dishonest and took all the profits for themselves; often they kept no accounts and no one was in a position to enforce the proper running of the farm. So in many cases the shareholders would do everything they could to get the loan repaid to enable the farm to be divided up into smallholdings. It was sad to see. Fine herds of dairy cows that had been bred up for many years by the former European owners would be sent to the meat factory, all the machinery would be sold, all water pumps, piping and fencing would be uprooted and even buildings would be dismantled and the materials sold off. Sometimes when the farm had been subdivided each shareholder would only get a very small portion, from one to three acres. As most African families are large, their houses would take up much of the land. If there happened to be any trees on the land, they would be cut down as crops will not grow under trees. Sometimes all the holder's money had gone into buying the land and he had no funds left to buy good seed and fertilizer. As it is not possible to use machinery on very small areas, the land would have to be prepared by hand. What cattle remained would be taken to graze alongside the roads or other land which was impossible to cultivate. Often these animals would have to walk long distances from home for food and water. All this meant that large productive farms became small subsistence holdings. Even worse, some of these farms were in low rainfall areas and had been stock farms, producing meat and wool, but became quite unproductive when put under maize, potatoes and beans. However, the new owners felt that so long as they owned a piece of land they could call their own, they had some security, and in a way they were right, for they would at least have somewhere to live if they became jobless or old.

On the other hand, there were some farms in parts of the country where there was high rainfall, with rich soil, and they did become productive when divided up and more intensively farmed, – occasionally even more productive than when they had been large-scale farms. Other large farms were bought by wealthy Africans and, when run well, continued to be as productive as before.

There was great rivalry among the people to get land. Aspiring politicians and other influential people would get a group together, collect money and start negotiations with landowners to buy their land.

Sometimes two groups would try for the same farm and this led to trouble and sometimes even violence. Money would be collected before an actual farm had been found; people often handed over all their savings, not always getting a receipt, and in many cases the money was never seen again. Often they did not know what kind of land they would be buying, but as long as they had land – any land – that was enough. Some unscrupulous people collected huge sums and kept it for themselves.

At Deloraine I would from time to time be visited by groups of people looking for land to buy. When they came, I used to tell them that I was not interested in selling, and usually they would leave without trouble, even though they would be very disappointed. But some were very insistent and would try again and again. Sometimes I received letters from lawyers or politicians asking if I wanted to sell. Often people would come and say: 'You have such a large bit of land, can't you let us have just a little bit?' Once or twice some women's group would come and suggest that they bought the farm and, as I was also a woman, I could be a member of the group! But I never had any real trouble with any of them. Sometimes I would hear rumours that people were collecting money to buy Deloraine even though it was not for sale, and I wondered if those who contributed ever got their money back.

Meanwhile life went on the same as before. It was sad when so many of my friends left the country; either they sold their farms or their jobs were 'Africanized'. On the other hand, new faces appeared, some of whom became good friends. New people, from different countries, brought with them fresh ideas and different points of view. Colonial society was inclined to be narrow-minded and stereotyped, even somewhat hide-bound, and it was like a breath of fresh air to meet a completely different set of people. Many of these people were 'experts' at this or that and would give one new ideas on various farming practices. Among these were some geneticists who were doing research on the Sahiwal cattle at the National Stud near Naivasha. They helped me considerably with a new line of development.

As the farm grew we had put in more water and fencing and started utilizing the rougher parts. I found that the Ayrshire cattle didn't thrive on the steeper hillsides, with the very coarse grass and a long walk to water. It was here the geneticists helped. I started crossing some of the Ayrshires with Sahiwals. These are Indian Zebu cattle and are a dual-purpose breed, unlike most Zebu cattle. We started by artificially inseminating some of the Ayreshire cows. The Sahiwal crosses made good steers as well as milkers and so we were able to utilize the rough land. Around 1965 I bought a small herd of pedigree Sahiwals and Deloraine has had a pedigree herd ever since.

Up to the time of the Mau Mau emergency, Kenya colony had to be self-supporting and everything had to be run as economically as possible. It wasn't until the emergency that any financial assistance from overseas was forthcoming. Once the country became independent, the situation became quite different. We were then classified as an 'under-developed country' and aid started to pour in. All kinds of schemes were started to improve the standard of living of the people and to develop the agricultural potential of the country. Kenya has to rely on agriculture, having few mineral or other assets. Schools and medical facilities increased tremendously, and tourism was encouraged. We are fortunate to have a lovely climate, as well as beautiful beaches and almost every kind of environment from sea to snowy mountain peaks, as well as lovely lakes and numerous species of birds and animals. The first National Parks had been started soon after the end of the Second World War and some lodges were built, which enabled people to see the wild life in comfort and ease. Animals soon became relatively tame, realizing that they would not be harmed in a park; in a car, people can come quite close to even the most dangerous animals, such as lions and elephants. Gradually tourism expanded until it was bringing in almost as much foreign exchange as agricultural exports.

Unfortunately, farming and wild life do not go well together. A farmer cannot allow wild animals free range over his land because they trample down and devour his crops as well as carrying infected ticks and diseases of all kinds to his domestic stock. So most of the game on farms has been shot, although some ranchers have made efforts to use some of their land, which is too hard and rough for cattle, to keep antelope such as oryx and eland on a commercial basis. On Deloraine we had originally some antelope and buffalo in the forest reserve behind the farm, and occasionally a leopard or hyena would kill a few cattle. Ever since I was a child I had wild animals as pets; Africans would bring in orphans that they had found for me to rear. Sadly, though, they usually had short lives and came to a bad end before long. Once a wild animal loses its fear of man and is taken out of its proper environment it doesn't know how to defend itself, and most of my pets were killed by predators, both human and animal. At one time I had a few eland that I got as small calves and I reared them with the cattle. The bull grew very large and strong and used actually to serve the Ayrshire cows but nothing ever came of it. He was full of racial prejudice and would only consort with the Ayrshires; he would have nothing to do with the Sahiwals! Perhaps this was because he had been suckled by an Ayrshire cow. Sometimes he fought the Ayrshire bulls and he could knock them down. After a while, however, he became a menace when he began chasing people and horning cows and I had to have him shot. Meanwhile the females started to have calves and wandered off onto another more open farm, a habitat such as they would have lived in had they been wild. Some people become very emotional about any wild animal and it used to amuse me, when I had English visitors, that they would be more interested in seeing these eland, which were quite useless creatures, than the highly productive dairy cows which I had bred up with such trouble and care over the years. There is a fascination with anything unusual.

I have reared antelope of different kinds, monkeys, ground squirrels and even a hyena, but of all the animals I have had I love the hyraxes best of all. They get very tame and are extremely intelligent. They are absolutely clean in the house and in fact they insist on using the W.C.! The only trouble with them is they will eat anything, including paper money and stamps, and they are much too fond of cigarettes and alcohol. One of mine got hepatitis from drinking too much sherry and I was told by the vet that he would have to give up the bottle. He would tip the bottle over so that it leaked and then suck up the drips. He could sit on a door handle and jump up and down until he had opened the door. They are, surprisingly, from the elephant family, their feet and skulls being built in the same manner. I had several that I loved very dearly but they would hop off for long safaris in the woods and sooner or later someone would meet my little friend and take him home for dinner. Once I was brought a pelt and was told: 'This must be Ebenezer, as the fur smells of your face powder.'

In 1964 I went to visit my Uncle John and Aunt Vi in their new home near Grasse in France. They had been forced to leave Hever, owing to some new English death duty laws which had bearing on the American Astor money: had they remained in Britain their family would have been virtually ruined. It was very sad to think that people who had done so much for Britain could no longer live there, but they made a beautiful home in France.

Moy and David, after his job had finished in Sweden, went to live in Oman for three years, where David commanded the Sultan's forces. Later they lived at Branxholme, the ancient Scott family castle near Hawick in the Borders, while the children were at school. During that time, David was in North Yemen for long periods, with the royalist guerrilla fighters.

At the end of the 1960s they bought some land in Spain and built themselves a house with some olive and almond farming land; but they returned to Britain in 1988. I visited them there twice. But I always come back to Deloraine.

In 1966 I went on a wonderful safari, starting in Ethiopia, which is a unique country, unlike anywhere else in Africa; from there I went on to Greece, which I found overwhelmingly beautiful, and after visiting France and Britain, I came home via Egypt, doing a trip up the Nile, wondering at all the Pharaonic relics, and the strange resemblances I kept seeing to customs, tools and weapons familiar in the traditional life of Kenya. Then I stayed a few days in Khartoum with some of the family of the Mahdi, who had fought the British at Omdurman.

I had often thought that it would be lovely to have somewhere of my own at the coast where I could go for a change from the farm. In 1968 I visited Lamu with my nephews, Xan and Philip Smiley, and we found an old Swahili house that the owner was willing to let on a long lease. Lamu is an island, one of an archipelago off the northern coast of Kenya, not far from the Somali border. The town is old, and the port in pre-colonial days used to be one of the most important on the East African coast. A lot of agricultural produce was shipped from there, as there was extensive farmland on the nearby mainland.

The East African coast had originally been peopled by Bantu-speaking people but later had been occupied by Arabs from Oman, Shirazis from Persia and other peoples who had settled and traded there for hundreds of years. They took wives and concubines from the local people, as well as from the slaves they had brought down from the interior. Then Vasco da Gama arrived in 1498 and the Portuguese took some of the coastal towns from the Arabs and some Portuguese settled and stayed. There had also been traders from the west coast of India for many years, and even some Chinese, and so the people of the coast, the Wa Swahili, have quite a mixture of blood. They are almost all Muslims but vary very much in appearance, some looking much more African than others.

The last slaves were only liberated in 1907. Although the slaves who were brought down from the interior suffered terribly on the journey, once they had been sold to their new owners and settled to work they usually lived in conditions that were not bad. Of course they had to do their master's bidding, but they usually lived more or less as the family and some were given great responsibilities and taught skills. The women were sometimes married by their owners and emancipated, when the slaves were eventually given their freedom, they often felt lost, having never had to fend for themselves, and they would beg their former owners to go on looking after them. But most of the big plantations that had been worked by slaves were abandoned and reverted to bush after slavery was abolished.

There are some beautiful buildings in the town, built by the Swahili people in a style quite unlike anywhere else, with beautiful plaster work and carved wooden doors. My house is one of these, although not very large. It is probably nearly two hundred years old. There is a mosque near called Mosikiti Nuru or the Shining Mosque. There are twenty-two mosques, in the town of about 8,000 people. The ladies wear the *buibui*, a black cloak, and cover their faces when they go out. The streets are very narrow, which keeps them cool as one side or the other is always in the shade. There are no cars on the island; you have to walk or go by donkey unless you take a boat. They still build the wooden sailing boats known as dhows, and these still ply to and from the Arabian Gulf, bringing dates and taking mangrove poles to Arabia for building, as there are few trees there.

I find it very relaxing to spend a few weeks there when I can. It is such a contrast with the farm, where I am rather isolated, to live in a street surrounded by people and to hear, as I lie in bed, the muezzin call the people to prayer before dawn.

By 1978, when I handed over, Deloraine was run entirely by Africans. There was an African manager, an African accountant and all the machinery, cattle records and general day-to-day running of the farm were looked after by Africans. Some of our workers were the third and fourth generation, descended from our original squatters, many of whom were still living on the farm. Our milking was all done by hand, so we employed a large number of milkers. Most of these were now Kalenjin and we had many fewer Masai than we used to, as their families and cattle have moved to Masai Mara and they do not come this way to look for work as they did. The young Masai these days wear T-shirts, fashionable trousers and shoes and play American pop music on their radios and tape recorders.

There are usually about a dozen young boys and girls from Deloraine in secondary schools or away doing training in different professions and every now and again I receive a postcard from some strange place, in Europe or Asia or America, from somebody who has gone there for further training. It is always a great pleasure to think that they have remembered me in such a distant land. Others come on a visit in their own motor cars and tell me about their jobs. I enjoy having Moy's sons to stay with me from time to time, and also her daughter Anna, who is a physiotherapist. She lived in Kenya for some years as she was married to a banker in Nairobi and her two children were born here. Gavin, Moy's eldest son, is in the Army, so was not able to visit me so often, but he and his wife and two sons come now and again when they can. So now five generations of our family have lived at Deloraine – my grandmother, Mary Minto, my parents, Moy and I, and Moy's children and grandchildren.

As the farm developed and there was more work to be done, I began to find this more and more of a responsibility and a tie. I was over sixty years of age when I was approached in 1978 by one of the Trustees of the Rift Valley College of Science and Technology, who asked whether I would sell shares in Deloraine to the College. I decided that it would be a good thing to do. I knew that they would continue to run the farm as before, and I made a stipulation that I should stay on in the house and rent back about sixty acres where I could keep a few cattle. We completed the deal in 1979.

At the time of handing over, the farm was over 5,000 acres. There were 1,700 head of cattle, about 350 of them being milked by hand, and 300 head of goats. The whole farm was fenced into paddocks and every paddock had water supplied to it. There were eighty-four kilometres of fencing, and about twenty-one kilometres of farm road.

On the day of handing over we had a party at Deloraine in my dining-room; we killed and roasted one of the goats and the new chairman drank my health and made a very nice little speech saying that they hoped that I would live happily there ever after in the surroundings and amongst the people I had known all my life.

Aged four, with mother and sister (foreground)

Lord Francis Scott (portrait by Oswald Birley) *As bridesmaid to Geraldine Macoun*

Deloraine

Home while the house was being built

With Moy's daughter and Masai

With spear, talking to Masai, 1941

At Deloraine, 1980

Index